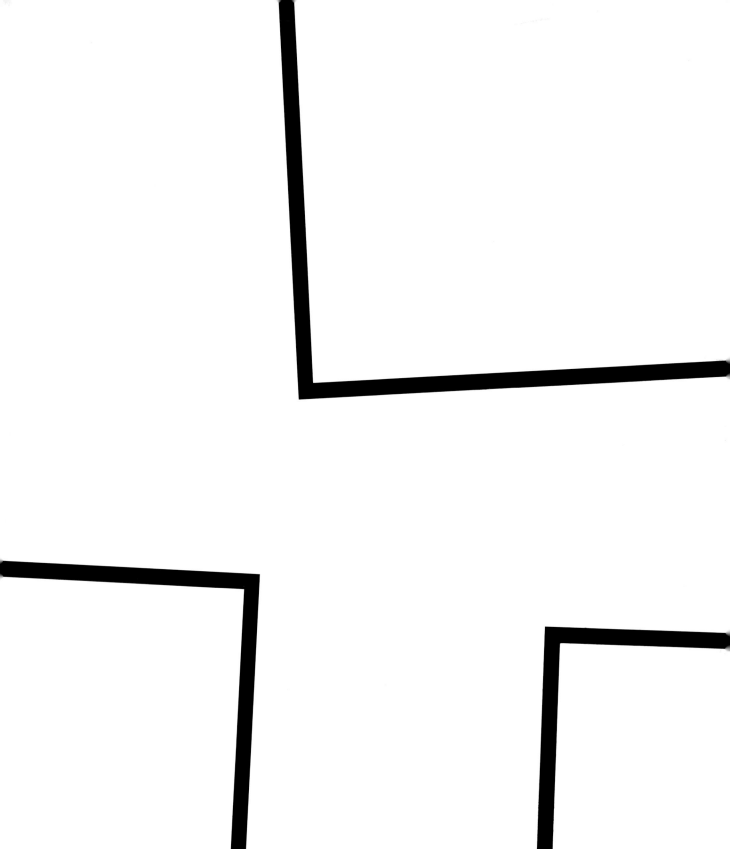

CONTEMPORARY FASHION STYLISTS

LUANNE MCLEAN

Published by Vivays Publishing Ltd
www.vivays-publishing.com

Every effort has been made to ensure that
the information was correct at the time of
going to press. Should any errors or omissions
be found please contact the publisher and we
will undertake to make such corrections, if
appropriate, but without prejudice.

A catalogue record for this book is
available from the British Library
ISBN 978-1-908126-18-4

Publishing Director: Lee Ripley
Design: Draught Associates

Printed in China

CONTENTS

INTRODUCTION

BEHIND EVERY FASHION SHOOT, BEHIND MANY OF THE EYE-CATCHING LOOKS TREADING THE RED CARPET ON OSCAR NIGHT, THERE IS A FASHION STYLIST HELPING HIS OR HER CLIENT TO LOOK FABULOUS. A GOOD STYLIST CAN FULFIL A BRIEF AT THE DROP OF A HAT TO CREATE THE REQUIRED LOOK; FROM PUTTING TOGETHER LOOKS FOR BUSINESS PEOPLE, FOR THEATRICAL PRODUCTIONS, MUSIC VIDEOS, TELEVISION AND FILM AND, OF COURSE, FOR THE BIGGEST THEATRE OF THEM ALL, THE CATWALK. STYLISTS COME IN ALL SHAPES AND FORMS AND THEIR WORK BEHIND THE SCENES HAS BEEN MORE WIDELY RECOGNISED IN RECENT YEARS. HERE WE EXPLORE WHAT A STYLIST ACTUALLY DOES, WHAT YOU NEED TO KNOW TO BECOME A STYLIST, AND HOW TO BE SUCCESSFUL IN THE EVER-CHANGING FASHION INDUSTRY, OPENING THE DOOR TO THE WORLD OF STYLING AND SHOWCASING THE MYSTERIES BEHIND CREATING THE RIGHT LOOK.

We speak to well known contemporary stylists working in all aspects of the industry and look at what it actually takes to be a celebrated stylist and answer the question how do these people create fantastic looks for the worlds of fashion, theatre and media? We will also ask their advice about how to get into the field and any tips they can offer about the profession.

Basically, a fashion stylist does the same thing that a hair or makeup artist does: they perfect a look and make their client feel sensational by giving them an overall sleek and groomed image—or wild and crazy image, depending on the occasion. Styling can be theatrical or purely original and creatively unique. In recent times, it has become increasingly popular to copy figures in the public eye. Most of us will have taken a picture to the hairdressers asking them to copy the latest trend and they will do their best to make you resemble that image. This is the basis of any good stylist--they create an optimum look to make their model, client or even themselves look fantastic for any given theme or occasion. Victoria Beckham is a perfect example. Copying the former Spice Girl's style was so widespread that she began her own fashion label and has become a respected and award-winning designer in her own right. Victoria's acceptance by the fashion industry shows her style has gone full circle from simply being copied to actually being created by her and she now dresses other women in the public eye.

STYLING BY COURTNEY SMITH

A STYLIST ESSENTIALLY FULFILS THE BRIEF OF MAKING THEIR CLIENT LOOK GOOD. THIS OFTEN INVOLVES CONSTRUCTING OUTFITS, ALTERING AND TAILORING ITEMS FOR THE PERFECT FIT, CUSTOMISING CLOTHES TO MAKE THEM MORE INDIVIDUAL AND EVEN COMMISSIONING DESIGNERS TO CREATE AN ITEM OF CLOTHING ESPECIALLY FOR THEIR CLIENT.

WHAT IS A STYLIST ?

Where would you find a stylist? Here are a few of the areas where the skills of the stylist are put to use:

Large department stores often have stylists and personal shoppers to aid customers with their purchases; everyone from busy lawyers to the mother of the bride can take advantage of this service.

ADVERTISING IS A HUGELY LUCRATIVE AREA OF STYLING – ALL BRANDS EMPLOY A STYLIST TO ENSURE THAT THEIR PRODUCT IS GIVEN THE CORRECT IMAGE FOR THEIR MARKET.

Editorial stylists ensure their publications' photo shoots and covers are perfectly styled from the model selected to the items worn and how they are combined.

WHAT IS A STYLIST ?

CATWALK STYLISTS HAVE SEVERAL OUTFIT CHANGES TO OVERSEE AND ENSURE THE AUDIENCE SEES EACH OUTFIT EXACTLY AS THE DESIGNER SKETCHED IT.

Music videos and concerts portray a certain look for a musician and each album or single campaign may have a different look to portray depending on the mood or theme of the song.

TELEVISION AND FILM STUDIOS HAVE HUGE WARDROBE DEPARTMENTS WHO ARE EMPLOYED TO DRESS THE CHARACTERS AND BRING THEIR PERSONALITIES TO LIFE.

Red carpet styling is essential to the look of an actress or personality and often a bad outfit can create bad publicity, especially at events such as the Oscars.

Employing a stylist who can create the correct look in any of these areas is key. Having someone who knows what is required in a certain situation can make the difference in how the public reacts to the client. Some stylists may specialise in one area such as the music industry, while others may work across all of the fields. Fashion is an incestuous industry and models often become stylists, as do public relations officers. Stylists may become designers themselves launching their own clothing lines like Rachel Roy, L'Wren Scott, and Misa Hylton-Brim. Building a network and interacting well with people are, therefore, key skills in this industry.

A BRIEF HISTORY OF STYLING

The term stylist first appeared in a magazine in the **1930's**. But styling has been around for centuries, for as long as people have worn clothes someone is in control of making sure that the "look" is produced and worn as imagined. During the Regency period of the **late 18th-early 19th centuries** great attention was paid to the way a neckcloth was tied, for example, and what it said about its wearer. A gentleman's valet might feel that his honour depended on his master appearing in public appropriately and stylishly dressed. In Napoleon Bonaparte's court, women were forbidden from wearing the same garment more than once. Perhaps not unlike red carpet appearances today? In certain circles image has always been important.

Indeed styling is simply that – creating an image formed in the imagination, bringing to life an idea of how the stylist would want someone to look. If given the same collection of clothes and accessories, every stylist would create a unique and varied image – no two would come up with the same outfit. Styling is about being an individual and responding to the individual client. Some stylists are accused of projecting their own personal styles onto their muses, others clearly use different inspirations each time without repeating a theme.

Stylists were much less significant in the fashion industry 50-years ago. The millennium became the turning point when stylists no longer remained obscure and faceless, but stepped into the spotlight. The role of the stylist is now deeply embedded in popular culture. In the modern world everywhere we go we are surrounded by visuals. Every time you encounter an image be it from a magazine, a TV show, a leaflet or an advertisement on a bus shelter, a creative team of authors have been involved in assembling that image to sell clothes or to put across a message. Stripped down to its most basic form a stylist puts clothes into the picture. But in reality they use fashion as a creative tool and can help generate visuals that define each decade using fashion as a means of expression.

In the golden age of Hollywood, stars like Marilyn Monroe and Rita Hayworth graced the red carpet, but the people behind their appearances might be unknown. The team of makeup, hair and styling artists who created their look remained faceless and nameless. Take Audrey Hepburn's character Holly Golightly in *Breakfast at Tiffany's* – who created that look? Whose idea was it to mix pearls and a cigarette holder with a classic black shift dress? Was it the legendary costume designer Edith Head or did someone else actually put together the dress with the accessories that created the iconic look? Now in the commercial Internet generation, the stylist for each celebrity

can often be famous in their own right and go on to produce their own clothing ranges, stores and even television shows featuring the everyday events of their job.

The boundaries between stylist and costume designer are sometimes very faint. A prime example is the aforementioned costume designer Edith Head who created looks for countless Hollywood films in addition to *Breakfast at Tiffany's* and received eight Academy Best Costume awards after an amazing 35 nominations, including accolades for the film

Sabrina in **1953**. On that production she worked closely with Givenchy to produce a celebrated and much copied 'Parisian' look. Starlets dressed by the cinematic stalwart during her **40's** and **50's** heyday included Ginger Rogers, Bette Davis, Shirley MacLaine, Grace Kelly and Elizabeth Taylor.

British fashion designer Mary Quant created some of the iconic looks of the **1960's** Mod movement. She is noted as being the creator of the miniskirt and her celebrated style was copied by young girls the world over. So although she was primarily a designer, she could be credited with styling a whole generation

into wearing a perfectly manicured bob, knee high boots and a shift dress. In the **1980's** Leigh Bowery crafted the look of bands such as Culture Club led by Boy George with men styled in outrageous outfits, portraying both genders and wearing makeup. Bowery styled and designed clothes that explored artistic expression and showed his wild imagination. Stylists often become involved in music and movements. The outrageous stage costumes of David Bowie and Michael Jackson have all been heavily copied. Stylist William Baker worked with Kylie Minogue towards the end of the **1990's** and became one of the first well-known music stylists, even releasing a book with Kylie chronicling their creations. In the current music scene, Nicki Minaj and Lady Gaga are both pushing fashion boundaries. Gaga's stylist Nicola Formichetti is the man behind the notorious meat dress, her outrageous hats and costumes for her Monster Ball tour. He is now one of the most sought after stylists of his generation.

Savvy celebrities realise the power stylists have to propel them into the limelight and often work very closely with their own stylists to produce the right image, in particular at high visibility events like the Oscars, the Golden Globe Awards and various music awards. Madonna is a master of manipulating public events to her advantage by using stylists who understand her. She has used a number of stylists for her various tours including Arianne Phillips who she has worked with for her last four tours and for her film W.E. Jean Paul Gaultier designed many of her stage costumes for the Blonde Ambition tour in **1990** including the famous conical bra.

Television and film are hugely influenced by fashion. Patricia Field is one stylist who changed the face of fashion on television, bringing high fashion to the masses as wardrobe mistress on *Sex and the City*. She brought her characters to life and spawned copycats all over the world who imitated the look of Carrie Bradshaw and her friends, mixing labels with vintage. Field went on to work on the acclaimed fashion film *The Devil Wears Prada* and launched her own fashion ranges as well as collaborating with British department store Marks and Spencer.

Rachel Zoe created a swarm of celebrity look-a-likes with her 'lollipop ladies'. Mischa Barton and Nicole Richie all became known for being styled by her with an oversized Balenciaga motorcycle bag and enormous bug-eyed sunglasses emphasising their small frames. Zoe, assistant Brad Goreski and her team then went on to have their own reality series showing the activity behind the scenes of their glamorous fashion lives.

STYLING BY
ANDREW CLANCEY

STYLING BY BIKI JOHN

In addition to Rachel Zoe's reality show, other styling shows on television have been very popular. Gok Wan showed British viewers how to customise their own clothes and Trinny and Susannah showed women 'what not to wear.' The Style Network has numerous television shows that cover fashion styles and styling.

In the world of high fashion and fashion magazines, many eclectic personalities create the looks depicted on the pages of magazines such as *Dazed and Confused* and, of course, *Vogue*. Über stylist Katie Grand and best friend Kate Moss's collaborations are legendary and her magazine *Love* is highly regarded. Grace Coddington once modelled for *Vogue* and now as creative director conceives the celebrated fashion spreads for American *Vogue*. Over at French *Vogue* when Carine Roitfeld was at the helm, shoots became more outrageous, and in 1996 her legendary 'butcher shoot' with photographer Mario Testino for *The Face* caused controversy. Fashion royalty Isabella Blow was credited with discovering the late great Alexander McQueen and became a stylist who inspired her generation. She was also known for her quirky hats and up front style.

While some stylists relish being in front of the camera, other stylists enjoy their anonymity and hide behind the images they create. Whether in the lime light or behind the scenes, there is much more awareness from the fashion-focussed public of stylists and the role they play as true visionaries who create beguiling and arresting images, which chronicle the times we live in.

ANATOMY OF A STYLING SESSION:
WHAT DOES A STYLIST DO?

Every styling session starts with a brief from the client and it is the stylist's role to interpret that brief and create the image that the client wants. The look the client has visualised in their imagination may be very specific or it may be more amorphous and difficult to convey. Often an initial consultation is set up so that the client can outline what they want, be it an advertising idea or a red carpet outfit. From this initial meeting the stylist can gain a better sense of what is expected from them.

For the next stage, the stylist researches the project and comes up with sketches, ideas and often mood boards to show the client. If everyone is in agreement about what is proposed, the stylist then sets about obtaining the clothing, props and accessories to fulfil the brief and liaising with the team he or she will be working with for the shoot. If the stylist creates what the client has envisioned, then the brief is fulfilled. Ultimately, a stylist makes the imaginings of the client a reality.

NOW LET'S LOOK AT WHAT HAPPENS AT AN ACTUAL STYLING SESSION.

THE BRIEF

I was asked to create a 'flower fairy' fashion shoot for an online company's publicity and advertising campaign. The shoot needed to appeal to the business's core market of 18-30 year old women and portray a fairy-like model lost in the woods in ethereal dresses.

On being given my brief, I initially brainstormed with the client about their ideas of fairies and what message they wanted to convey. I then searched for images of fairies so that I could recreate the colours, the poses, the lighting and the light-as-a-feather dresses in my own shoot. After looking at a wide range of fairy images and models posed as fairies, I began researching dresses both full length and cropped as well as accessories that would complement a natural fairy look.

INSPIRATIONAL MOOD BOARD IMAGES FOR A "FLOWER FAIRY LOST IN A FOREST" THEME

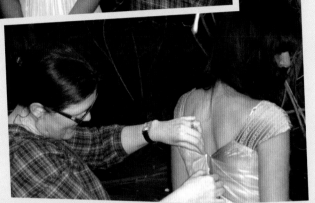

ANATOMY OF A STYLING SESSION:
WHAT DOES A STYLIST DO?

THE MODEL AND LOCATION

Next I needed to find a location for the shoot. A beautiful woodland with sculpted tree stumps and a well-lit clearing proved to be the perfect place to stage our shoot and I cast a tanned, long-limbed model with long, flowing natural black hair to emulate my fairy poses.

CREATING THE STYLE

In styling the model, I had to take into account all the elements of her appearance to successfully create the look I wanted: from her well manicured bare feet in some shots to the way her hair flowed in the wind, making sure that underwear and bra straps were hidden from view and that the pictures looked relaxed and used the light well.

Adding accessories to the dress and her hair gave the look authenticity, but with accessories less is often more. I had to try out a few options with each dress to figure out what would look best.

FROM THE TOP, STYLING THE MODEL ON THE SHOOT SET, HIDING VISIBLE STRAPS, PINNING THE BACK OF AN ILL FITTING DRESS AND BELOW A WINNING POSE

FROM THE TOP, TRYING OUT DIFFERENT ACCESSORIES, ADJUSTING A HAIR CLIP AND BOTTOM GIVING A HELPING HAND TO CLIMB A TREE TRUNK TO ACHIEVE THIS FINAL POSE

STYLING BY
LUANNE MCLEAN

THE SHOOT

The outfits themselves had to look good, so the photographer and I chose areas of the wood that were well lit, but still portrayed our ethereal theme.

The photographer took a number of test shots before she was satisfied that she had the poses and effects that were wanted. The shoot was also interrupted when an unexpected guest in the form of a rather lively dog decided he wanted to be part of the shoot and had to be escorted back to his owner.

Finally numerous photographs were taken and the photographer and I were satisfied that we had a range of images to choose from. We then studied those images to pick out the ones we thought fulfilled our brief best.

This part is often very difficult – one shoot can comprise over a hundred shots, but only a handful make the final editorial or in this case advertising spread. Art directors, photographers and stylists all have different opinions and by expressing these and keeping the brief and client's market in mind, the shots are whittled down to a final selection.

THE OUTCOME

After making our final choices, it was time to present the pictures to the client at a final meeting. At this session, the end use of the pictures is discussed along with which pictures are more suitable for a print advertising campaign and which should be sent out as part of the email marketing. The images chosen are essential for communicating to the customer what type of brand my client represents and if the client feels that the shoot will accomplish this, then it is considered to be a success. I feel the final shots fulfil my brief perfectly and together as a creative team we depicted a modern day fairy story ideally matched to my client's core customer. The client agrees.

THE FINAL STAGE

After the shoot, the clothing samples and accessories need to be returned to the shops and PR companies from which they have been borrowed. This is an essential, but sometimes tedious, task often given to interns. But it is a great way of making contacts and learning the names and addresses of the PRs for certain brands. All samples should be sent back promptly -usually within 7 days- folded neatly and in the condition they were received.

FINAL IMAGES FROM THE SHOOT
TO FULFILL BY CLIENTS BRIEF OF A
FLOWER FAIRY THEME FOR THEIR
ADVERTISING CAMPAIGN

MODEL CARLA CRESSY
PHOTOGRAPHY BY TRACY MORTER
STYLING BY LUANNE MCLEAN

HOW TO
BECOME A
STYLIST

THERE IS NO ONE PRESCRIBED WAY TO BECOME A STYLIST. WHILE SOME STYLISTS MIGHT HAVE STUDIED FASHION DESIGN OR FASHION RETAILING AT COLLEGE OR UNIVERSITY, OTHERS STARTED AS INTERNS, LEARNING THEIR CRAFT ON THE JOB. STILL OTHERS SEEM TO HAVE FALLEN INTO THE INDUSTRY FROM A COMPLETELY DIFFERENT CAREER PATH AND DISCOVER THAT STYLING IS WHAT THEY REALLY WANT TO DO.

HERE I HAVE ASKED A RANGE OF TOP FASHION STYLISTS THEIR ADVICE ON MAKING A CAREER IN FASHION STYLING...

Be available – whenever, wherever - styling isn't a 9 to 5 job! Early mornings and late nights are both common

Learn how to work in a team and hone your craft with up and coming photographers and models who also need to build up their portfolios by doing lots of test shoots to show off your skills.

Always have an open mind, be curious, and ask questions about everything.

Be passionate – practice! You don't have much money to start with so you have to love what you do.

Don't complain. It's not always glamorous--returns and invoicing come hand-in-hand with the job.

Take a fashion course to ensure you have a good basic knowledge and that this is the right industry for you.

You really have to be trustworthy in order to look after the clothes, accessories and jewellery you are loaned.

To embark on a fashion stylist career, you must be prepared to do a lot of assisting and interning jobs that are unpaid. It is important to learn on the job when it comes to styling – experience is key.

Try the unexpected, explore and be creative.

Don't be afraid to ask designers and shops if you can borrow clothes.

Show your creativity and your personality in your work.

GIVE YOURSELF TIME. IT DOESN'T HAPPEN OVERNIGHT.

STYLING BY, L-R, CRYSTAL
DEROCHE AND ELAUAN LEE

THE KNOWLEDGE

WHAT EVERY STYLIST NEEDS TO KNOW

PRACTICAL STYLING TOOLS YOU
NEED TO INVEST IN ...

&

SKILLS AND KNOWLEDGE YOU
NEED TO DEVELOP...

As every stylist will tell you, there are certain things
you need to know and certain tools you have to own
to be a successful stylist. As a starting point, a stylist
must have a strong sense of colour and a flair for
fashion. Communication skills and the ability to build
relationships are absolutely essential; you need to be
able to listen to the client and to interpret their
brief to your team.

THE KNOWLEDGE

WHAT EVERY STYLIST NEEDS TO KNOW

Below is the list of what every stylist needs to know.
This covers a range of areas from practical styling tools you need
to invest in to skills and knowledge you need to develop.

STYLING KIT

The most essential thing for a stylist to take to any assignment! Your kit must include- safety pins and dress pins, sewing kit, nude underwear and matching bra, nude and black tights, tit tape, a lint roller, scissors and a few accessories (hair bands, clips, brooches, bracelets)

CONTACT BOOK

This is a must – an address book with all fashion PR's, shops, photographers, models and make-up artists' contact numbers in it. Make sure you keep it up to date as the world of fashion is ever changing and PR's move around constantly.

RESEARCH

Before every job do the research on your client or model, theme and location so there are no surprises on the day! Moodboards are helpful at the shoot planning stage.

BODY SHAPE AWARENESS

Not everything suits every body, the first time you meet a client decide what shape they are: pear, apple, hourglass or boyish. This will guide you to what will suit their body shape.

VINTAGE

Vintage fashion is something that has become very popular in recent times and any good stylist should know where to find vintage gems if their client's criteria require it.

TRENDS

Seasonal and fashion trend knowledge is a must – what's in, what's available and what should be avoided.

COLOUR MATCHING

A stylist must know how to mix colours well be it for a clashing look or a smart look. Colour blocking is currently very popular.

DESIGNER AND HIGH STREET KNOWLEDGE

Fashion changes everyday – new collaborations, new stores, and new designers and, unfortunately, in the current climate some shops are no longer around. Knowing which are the best stores for a certain look and what they stock is invaluable.

ONLINE RETAILERS

Online fashion stores now generate more sales than the high street and bulk orders to these shops save a poor stylist's feet. You need to factor in delivery times, however, so it may not possible to order on-line for assignments with a short lead time.

A GOOD QUALITY SUITCASE

All samples need to be well looked after so a good quality, lightweight, wheeled suitcase is essential. Always return samples in good condition

A STEAMER

Samples need to be ironed and look perfect, so ensure you have a hand steamer available. All clothes should be crease free and look their best.

STYLING BY, L-R, LIZZI ZITA
AND HERSHEY PASCUAL

PROFESSIONAL 12 TIPS

STYLED BY CRYSTAL DEROCHE

THERE IS NO ONE PRESCRIBED WAY TO BECOME A STYLIST. WHILE SOME STYLISTS MIGHT HAVE STUDIED FASHION DESIGN OR FASHION RETAILING AT COLLEGE OR UNIVERSITY, OTHERS STARTED AS INTERNS, LEARNING THEIR CRAFT ON THE JOB. STILL OTHERS SEEM TO HAVE FALLEN INTO THE INDUSTRY FROM A COMPLETELY DIFFERENT CAREER PATH AND DISCOVER THAT STYLING IS WHAT THEY REALLY WANT TO DO.

HERE I HAVE ASKED A RANGE OF TOP FASHION STYLISTS THEIR ADVICE ON MAKING A CAREER IN FASHION STYLING...

1

'Practice styling to build up a portfolio, work with different people and concepts'

CRYSTAL DEROCHE

PROFESSIONAL · TIPS

'Research is a very important part of our work, know your fashion history and style but also look into what different continents, eras and cultures have to offer.'

CARMEN HAID

2

STYLED BY CARMEN HAID

3

'A degree in
styling isn't
necessary,
just do it'

ELAUAN LEE

PROFESSIONAL · TIPS

STYLED BY COURTNEY SMITH

4

'Work your butt off. If that fails, work harder!'

COURTNEY SMITH

PROFESSIONAL · TIPS

STYLED BY BIKI JOHN

5

'Join the website Whoistesting.com a London-based site dedicated to fashion and beauty photographers, stylists, and hair and makeup artists from around the UK and worldwide who are actively testing. Having had no official stylist training, qualifications or contacts when I began styling, this site helped me meet a community of like-minded people and my first test with a photographer on this site landed me my first front cover and published work, and the rest as they say is history.'

BIKI JOHN

6

'Be ambitious'

HERSHEY PASCUAL

PROFESSIONAL · TIPS ·

'Develop a reputation and work on building strong relationships with fashion PR companies by always attending launches and returning their calls and samples!'

LIZZI ZITA

7

STYLED BY LIZZI ZITA

8

'Believe in
the power of
collaboration'

COURTNEY SMITH

STYLED BY COURTNEY SMITH

'Always have
an open mind,
be curious,
explore, and ask
questions about
everything.'

FARAH KABIR

9

PROFESSIONAL · TIPS

PROFESSIONAL'S TIP

'Always remind the model to wear nude underwear! They WILL forget.'

ROSA OSPINA

10

STYLED BY ROSA OSPINA

PROFESSIONAL · TIPS

11

'To become a stylist do what comes naturally to you, don't copy someone else, resonate your personality and what comes from within. Copying is not style.'

ALEXIA SOMERVILLE

'Take care of your credit and learn some accounting skills. You need to have credit cards to shop.'

CHIARA SOLLOA

12

PROFESSIONAL · TIPS ·

STYLED BY CHIARA SOLLOA

THE
PROFILES

In this section we explore the styling profession in all of its variants. The twenty stylists profiled here represent a wide range of approaches and backgrounds. Some style for the music industry, others for catwalk fashion; some specialise in red carpet glamour and still others work in several areas of the fashion industry.

The following profiles give an insight into the careers and portfolios of some of the most successful contemporary stylists working today.

Each profile tells you a bit about the background and training of the stylist and a glimpse into the life of the stylist and their plans. Each stylist offers practical advice both on how to get into the business and what you need to know as you are starting out. From hip hop to runway, from subdued to outrageous these international stylists demonstrate that creating the right look can be done in so many ways.

LUPE CASTRO

ANDREW CLANCEY

KHALIAH CLARK

JOEL DASH

CRYSTAL DEROCHE

CARMEN HAID

BIKI JOHN

FARAH KABIR

ELAUAN LEE

ZOE LEM

ARIETA MUJAY

ROSA OSPINA

HERSHEY PASCUAL

NIKKI PENNIE

KALVIN RYDER

ANGELA SCANLON

COURTNEY SMITH

CHIARA SOLLOA

ALEXIA SOMERVILLE

LIZZI ZITA

THE
STYLISTS

LUPE CASTRO

Brief Biography

SPANISH-BORN LUPE TRAINED IN COLOUR AND STYLE AT ASTON & HAYES, LONDON, AND CURRENTLY WORKS AS AN INDEPENDENT ETHICAL STYLIST AS WELL AS A BRAND CONSULTANT AND FREELANCE WRITER, FOCUSING ON NEW AND UPCOMING LABELS IN THE FASHION INDUSTRY. SHE ALSO WORKED AS A BRAND AGENT AND BUYER FOR SEVEN YEARS. LUPE'S PORTFOLIO INCLUDES ORGANISING SHOOTS FOR MAGAZINES SUCH AS *NATIONAL GEOGRAPHIC GREEN*, *EGGMAG* AND STYLING FOR BOTH PUBLIC AND PRIVATE EVENTS AND FASHION SHOWS FOR FUTURES 100, DAISY GREEN, AND UK AWARE, MOLTON HOUSE. SHE SOURCES INFORMATION ON ETHICAL FASHION FOR THE PRESS AND RETAILERS AND WAS A KEY MEMBER OF THE BIGWARDROBE.COM, BIG SWISH EVENTS LONDON AND FOUNDER OF ETHICALHEAVEN.COM. SHE WAS ALSO PART OF THE TEAM IN THE FIRST ECOLUXE EVENTS AT FASHION WEEK. LUPE IS DEEPLY COMMITTED TO ETHICAL FASHION, WHICH MEANS CLOTHING THAT IS PRODUCED IN A WAY THAT HAS A MINIMAL IMPACT ON DWINDLING RESOURCES.

AN ELEGANT LINGERIE SHOOT
STYLED BY LUPE CASTRO

HOW DID YOU GET INTO THE FIELD?

Through working with photographers and also through my experience of being a fashion agent and styling for shoots, window displays and image consultancy.

DO YOU HAVE ANY TIPS FOR BUDDING STYLISTS?

Contacts, contacts, contacts! Get yourself about. Volunteer for shoots and portfolios.

Make sure you make up a good portfolio, with lots of different styles, including catalogue, music, night and day, include lots of varying styles to make yourself marketable.

WHAT ARE YOU CURRENTLY DOING?

Lupe is currently traveling throughout Europe, Canada, New Zealand and Central America, on the back of a motorbike (and perhaps a plane or two and the odd boat, and a car), driven by a man we'll know simply as, Mr P, and with only a very small compartment for her clothes, shoes, accessories and makeup. Along the way she will visit and stylishly report on the famous food festivals in Spain, the sumptuous boutiques dotting France and the exotic cultures of Central America. Her travel diary can be followed at Mscastroonamotorbike.com

A HIGH GLAMOUR FASHION IMAGE WITH THE MODEL LITERALLY DROWNING IN HANDBAGS

WHAT ACHIEVEMENT ARE YOU MOST PROUD OF?

Very hard to call. It's a toss up between doing individual styling on a couple of clients who I thought were going to be impossible, or getting up on a stage and compering a catwalk show without preparation in front of 800 people and not faltering!

WHICH PUBLICATIONS HAVE YOU WORKED WITH?

EggMag, National Geographic Green, Daisy Green Magazine, WWB, Mode Affaire, Green My Style (Greenmystyle.com)

WHAT ARE YOUR FUTURE PLANS?

I have a couple of things in the pipeline mainly a book and a show, but currently I am concentrating on travelling and am determined to ride to Mongolia - the textiles and scenery are reputedly out of this world!

MS CASTRO ON A MOTORBIKE

(FAR LEFT) LUPE RELAXING
BETWEEN SHOOTS, HER CURRENT
PROJECT IS HER TRAVEL BLOG
WRITTEN WHILST TOURING THE
WORLD ON A MOTORCYCLE
AND (ABOVE AND RIGHT) LUPE'S
STYLING FOR HIGH-OCTANE
MENSWEAR

ANDREW CLANCEY

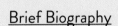

www.anyoldiron.net

ANYOLD
IRON
New York

149 ORCHARD STREET
NEW YORK NY 10002
PH +1 212-254-4404
FAX +1 212-254-4414
WWW.ANYOLDIRON.NET

Brief Biography

NEW YORK-BASED ANDREW CLANCEY TOOK AN INTERESTING ROUTE INTO FASHION. HE WENT FROM TRUCK DRIVING IN YORKSHIRE TO BECOMING A BRITISH FASHION ADVOCATE IN NEW YORK. ANDREW AND HIS SISTER, JULIA STEPPED INTO THE FASHION LIMELIGHT WHEN JULIA'S DESIGNS TOOK OFF AND ANDREW STYLED HER WORK. HE THEN WENT ON TO DO CAMPAIGNS FOR HUGE BRANDS SUCH AS SPECSAVERS AND FRONT COVERS FOR SEVERAL MAGAZINES INCLUDING A SPACEMAN THEMED SHOOT WITH SIR RICHARD BRANSON.

HE OWNS THE DESIGNER BOUTIQUE ANY OLD IRON, WHICH IS BASED ON THE LOWER EAST SIDE OF NEW YORK CITY AND SPECIALISES IN BRITISH MENSWEAR. ANDREW BRINGS EDGY NEW BRITISH DESIGNER WEAR TO NY CUSTOMERS.

FROM TOP ANDREW SHOWING OFF HIS COLOURFUL PERSONAL STYLE, A FLIER FROM HIS BOUTIQUE, ANY OLD IRON, AND ENJOYING A LAUNCH PARTY

HOW DID YOU GET INTO THE FIELD?

Andrew started by assisting his sister, fashion designer Julia Clancey. Julia launched her own fashion label in 2003 and regularly participates in London Fashion week. He went on to work as fashion editor at *Large* magazine, where his sister was also editor, before having a successful freelance career styling celebrities for music videos and album covers. He has done work with the music industry for brands such as the Ministry of Sound and Dizzee Rascal, as well as editorial spreads for magazines and advertising campaigns.

DO YOU HAVE ANY TIPS FOR BUDDING STYLISTS?

Assist for a year then become a stylist, go out to all the events, launches, fashion shows and parties. Getting to know the PR over a glass of wine is much better than training at a fashion college, as you get your name known and build up good relationships. It's all about contacts, being able to ring up people 20 minutes before a shoot and say I need this and that.

ANDREW STYLED THIS QUIRKY ACCESSORY SHOOT

ANDREWS' MODEL CAUSES
A FASHION RIOT

CAN YOU GIVE US A BRIEF
OVERVIEW OF WHAT YOU DO?

Andrew is a freelance fashion stylist who is truly passionate about his work. He is known for styling album covers for Dizzee Rascal's *Boy in Da Corner* album and his work with Basshunter. He also styles for magazines such as *Guitar Aficionado* and *Large*.

Two years ago he opened his New York-based store, Any Old Iron. He is very involved with the day to day running of the shop; from buying in clothes to merchandising, right down to working on the shop floor dealing with customers. Any Old Iron's stock is predominantly from British labels and has an edgy feel with labels like Red Mutha and was the first stockist in NYC of Delusion. Andrew has clients all over America, for whom he acts as stylist and personal shopper.

WHO ARE YOUR MAIN CLIENTS
AND PUBLICATIONS?

Ministry of Sound – around 8 album covers, Basshunter, Club Sky, TV adverts, Specsavers national advertising campaign, *Guitar Aficionado*, *Large* magazine, Mahogany Hair salon in London. He styled for Mahogany at the Royal Albert Hall for the Alternative Hair awards. Julia Clancey's runway shows.

WHICH ACHIEVEMENTS ARE YOU
MOST PROUD OF?

Opening up Any Old Iron is the greatest achievement. I enjoy taking humorous British styles such as Vivienne Westwood's to America. I buy stock in my own taste and am proud to share my eclectic style with my customers.

Also the Alternative Hair Awards at the Royal Albert Hall, where I do art direction for the runway shows was a huge accolade.

KHALIAH CLARK

www.khaliaclark.com

(ABOVE) KHALIAH ADDING
FINISHING TOUCHES TO COSTUME
STYLING AND MAKEUP ON SET
AND (RIGHT) SPORTSMAN BRUCE
JOHNSON NFL PLAYER OF THE
NY GIANTS

Brief Biography

KHALIAH CLARK IS US-BASED AND
HAS BEEN WORKING IN THE FASHION
INDUSTRY SINCE 1999. STARTING
AS A SALES REP FOR FULL FORCE
SALES WITH OZZIE STEWART, SHE HAS
WORKED FOR CLOTHING LINES SUCH
AS BUSTA RHYMES' BUSHI, KARL KANI,
AND THE RUFF RYDERS' DIRTY DENIM
COLLECTION.

IN 2001, KHALIAH MOVED ON TO
WORK WITH BALLA APPAREL, ONE OF
THE LEADING LINES IN URBAN WEAR.
AT BALLA, SHE TOOK ON A VARIETY OF
RESPONSIBILITIES, FROM BEING SHOW
ROOM MANAGER, TO ASSISTING THE
VP OF MARKETING IN ALL PRODUCT
PLACEMENTS, TO CONTRIBUTING TO
MATTERS OF PUBLIC RELATIONS. AS
A VALIDATION OF HER HARD WORK,
KHALIAH WAS INVITED TO HOST THAT
YEAR'S FIRST EVER URBAN FASHION
WEEK IN MIAMI.

Ready for a change, she moved on to work for Baby Phat in 2003. Interning first for the VP of Public Relations, Khaliah was involved in all facets of the fashion business, including product placement, visual merchandising, production, and styling. Khaliah worked on both the spring and fall season lines, and in 2004 she was named venue manager for the Kimora Lee Simmons Fashion Show at Radio City Music Hall in New York.

Wishing to expand the reach of her work, Khaliah jumped at the opportunity to work for the critically acclaimed independent film, *My Brother*. Her work as Wardrobe Supervisor provided her with valuable experience in the field of fashion in film.

In May 2005, Khaliah once was again honored with the pleasure of working with Urban Fashion Week, this time as Event Coordinator for the two-day Urban Fashion Main Event in New York. Held in a Westside loft in Manhattan, the event showcased some of the hottest brands in fashion, such as Baby Phat, Akademiks,

Def Jam University, Azzure, Ecko Red, and Phat Farm. Currently, Khaliah does freelance work as a fashion stylist, event coordinator, and production consultant, as well as projects with fashion extraordinaire Roger McKenzie and his agency Brat Pack, Inc. As the First Lady of Brat Pack, Khaliah has worked with an amazing list of celebrities, stylists and TV shows. She has worked with outstanding stylists such as legendary stylist June Ambrose who she assisted on the Rocawear campaign, Ne Yo's "Go On Girl", Pamela Watson on T-Pain, Method Mad and Eric Santiago on Burning Spears. She has worked with celebrities such as Mya, R. Kelly, Method Man, Carmen Electra, American Idol's Paris Bennett, gospel sensation Nyoki, rock legend Joan Jett, and reggae pioneer Burning Spear. As for TV, Khaliah has done work with MTV's TRL, BET's 106 and Park, Jimmy Kimmel Live, VH1's The White Rapper Show, and most recently she has styled one of the stars of HBO's *The Wire*, J.D. Williams, while continuing to gather clients and garner a reputation as one of today's top stylist.

L-R BRUCE JOHNSON OF NY
GIANTS AND LARRY ENGLISH OF
THE SAN DIEGO CHARGERS BOTH
AS STYLED BY KHALIAH CLARK

ANY TIPS FOR BUDDING STYLISTS?

Rule number 1: Study your craft,
know everything there is about styling.
Every day you should be learning
something new!

Rule number 2: Keep yourself
indispensable.

Rule number 3: Most important,
LISTEN always LISTEN,
and keep notes.

HOW DID YOU GET INTO THIS FIELD?

I came into this business as an intern
for Roger McKenzie.

WHICH ACHIEVEMENT ARE YOU MOST PROUD OF?

Being a mother, but in styling my proudest achievement has been working with those who inspire me like June Ambrose, Misa Hiton and Lisa Hilson, my icon in fashion. Overall, I am proud of just being in this business and continuing to work in what I love - styling.

WHO ARE YOUR MAIN CLIENTS?

I›m a freelancer so I have many clients, not just one main client but to name a few: rapper Hazel E, rapper Santa, Bruce Johnson (NFL Giants player). I am working with a slew of other people, running a business with Joe eXclusive's Destination 1610.

I am working with my nephew's clothing line The Clark Boyz making them the industry-leading brand. I also co-host a radio talk show THE CHOP SHOP every Monday on pncradio.com, and I want to give a mega shout out to Shampoo and YVCS, and DJ Furious.

PLANS FOR THE FUTURE?

I plan on expanding what I am doing with my new business partner Joe eXclusive of Destination 1610 and styling more of the industry's biggest names. I also want to expand on my team, starting with Geneva Relf who helps me with research and features. I would like to do more work on films and in costuming. I'm really working more on that this year. But you can find me on twitter @kc_ynvs and Facebook - Khaliah Clark my website is www.khaliahclark.com

JOEL
DASH

www.thedashempire.com

Brief Biography

AFTER ACCIDENTALLY FALLING INTO
THE FASHION INDUSTRY, JOEL STARTED
HIS BLOG WWW.THEDASHEMPIRE.COM
IN AUGUST 2009.

HE DEVELOPED A CULT FOLLOWING
WHO FELL IN LOVE WITH HIS FASHION
INSIDER POSTS ON PARTIES, SHOWS
AND MUST-HAVE LUXURY GOODS.
HE SOON FOUND HE WAS MUCH
SOUGHT AFTER FOR WORK AS A
WARDROBE STYLIST AND IMAGE
CONSULTANT FOR STARS OF MUSIC,
TV, AND THEATRE AND FOR FASHION
RUNWAY SHOWS,

(LEFT), R'N'B DIVA KELLY
ROWLAND AND (TOP RIGHT),
SEEING DOUBLE ITS JOEL HIMSELF

HOW DID YOU GET INTO THE FIELD?

To be honest I sort of fell into it.
I'd actually studied law and psychology
originally in the hope of becoming a
barrister. However after interning at
a punk magazine at the beginning of
my career, which wasn't necessarily
'high fashion', it introduced me to the
industry and I made friends with some
amazing people who helped me realize
that I had a keen eye for detail.
So what was supposed to be a
summer internship turned out
to be so much more!

(FAR LEFT) CREATING RED
CARPET GLAMOUR FOR
GLEE STAR AMBER RILEY
(ABOVE RIGHT AND BELOW)
NICKI HITS THE STAGE AND
FASHION SHOWS IN JOEL'S
EYE CATCHING OUTFITS

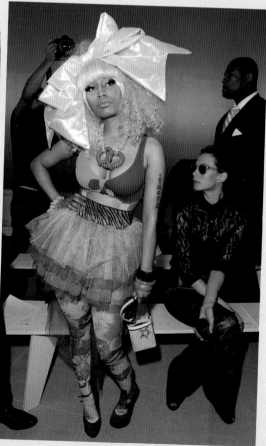

ANY TIPS FOR BUDDING STYLISTS?

Keep your eyes wide-open, ears clean, mouth shut! Be prepared to work 20-hour days for a week straight. Don't complain.

WHAT ACHIEVEMENT ARE YOU MOST PROUD OF?

Working with Nicki Minaj on 'Good Morning America', the Grammys, and her phenomenal *Billboard* Award performance in May 2011 and recent tour with Britney Spears. Also, working with Kelly Rowland on her first session of UK X-Factor.

WHO ARE YOUR MAIN CLIENTS AND PUBLICATIONS?

Kelly Rowland, Nicki Minaj, and most recently Amber Riley (Mercedes from Glee). Publications worked for: *In Style*, *Wallpaper**, *Esquire*.

WHAT ARE YOUR FUTURE PLANS?

Top secret!

BELOW) GIVING KELLY ROWLAND A STYLISH ENSEMBLE AND SOPHISTICATED AWARD'S GLAMOUR

CRYSTAL
DEROCHE

www.crystalderoche.co.uk

(RIGHT AND OPPOSITE) CRYSTAL
USES ELABORATE JEWELLERY AND
COLOURFUL PRINTS TO CREATE
HER AFRICAN INSPIRED LOOKS

Brief Biography

CRYSTAL IS A FREELANCE FASHION STYLIST WHO WORKS ON COMMISSIONED ASSIGNMENTS AROUND THE WORLD AND IS KNOWN FOR HER FLAIR IN STYLE AND FASHION. CRYSTAL WAS BORN AND RAISED IN PARIS. HER PARENTS WERE ORIGINALLY FROM LAGOS AND SHE GREW UP WITHIN A VERY SMALL NIGERIAN COMMUNITY THERE AND WAS EXPOSED TO VARIOUS OTHER AFRICAN CULTURES (E.G., IVORIAN, CAMEROONIAN, SENEGALESE, ETC.). SHE CAME FROM A LARGE FAMILY WITH FOUR BROTHERS. HER PARENTS WERE VERY SUPPORTIVE OF ANYTHING SHE WANTED TO GET INVOLVED IN, SPORTS, ARTS, YOU NAME IT.

WORKING ON BOTH EDITORIAL AND COMMERCIAL PHOTO-SHOOTS, SHE ALSO DOES VIDEOS AND TV ADVERTISEMENTS. CRYSTAL HAS DONE CATWALK SHOWS SUCH AS LONDON FASHION WEEK, NSPCC FUNDRAISERS, TMC AND "ELEGANCE" FASHION SHOWS TO NAME A FEW. SHE HAS DEVELOPED STRONG RELATIONSHIPS WITH DESIGNERS AND PR AGENCIES, AND IS ALWAYS LOOKING FOR NEW AND CHALLENGING PROJECTS. CRYSTAL'S VISION OF STYLE LIES IN A MIXTURE OF SHAPES, TEXTURE AND COLORS, WHICH ALLOW HER TO CREATE ORIGINAL PIECES FOR EDITORIAL STORIES.

HOW DID YOU GET INTO THE FIELD?

I was lucky enough to be involved in the fashion world at a very young age. My parents owned two boutiques in Paris. Through them I learned a lot about body shapes, skin tones, colours and textures. It was always a pleasure to me to help guide clients in their choices and so I became a personal stylist for many of our regular clients.

I had always been interested in branding and its effect on consumers so I did a degree in business administration with a specialization in marketing. After getting my degree, I decided to go to London to pursue an international career. While in London, I was recruited by an international research company as a communications executive. I worked with the company for five years and still regularly travel between Paris and London.

At first I did styling work on a part-time basis when friends requested my help, however the demand started to grow and in 2008 I decided to do styling full time.

My first editorial spread was for an international fashion and lifestyle magazine called *Sublime*. It was an amazing experience. Working with the photographer to create the concept and the theme of this editorial was very exciting. I was given the opportunity to be extremely creative as the theme of the brief was 'the future'. I decided, therefore, to source garments with different shapes and different textures to create my interpretation of the theme.

The biggest obstacle was leaving my job and starting my fashion styling business. It was a very risky decision at the time, as the recession had just started and people where fighting to keep their jobs in order to secure regular income for their families.

WHAT WERE YOUR QUALIFICATIONS IN THE FIELD?

No formal training in styling per se, but she had hands-on experience of working in her parents' two boutiques; one selling ready-to-wear and another specialising in evening wear. Crystal was familiar with buying for the shops and styling the clients from an early age.

ANY TIPS FOR BUDDING STYLISTS?

Practice styling to build up a portfolio, work with different people and concepts on test shoots, work with different themes and always intensely research these. When planning a shoot, my multi-cultural background, music, movies, books and also art in various forms inspire me.

Be passionate but practical as there is not much money to start with.

CAN YOU GIVE US A BRIEF OVERVIEW OF WHAT YOU DO?

I freelance as well as working through agencies. I like diversity in what I do from creative magazine spreads, to fashion shows to exhibitions.

My favourite part of the job is interpreting the brief from clients. I really enjoy coming up with concepts and planning meetings with the PRs in order to select the pieces that will allow me to create my vision.

The worst part of the job has to be dropping off all the garments and accessories that were used. It can take a long time if you try to do it all yourself. Assistants are definitely a must-have as they not only help you, but also learn from you.

TWO CONTRASTING SHOOTS, ON THIS PAGE ONE WITH A SLEEK CITYSCAPE SET AND OPPOSITE A SHOOT THAT IS TEXTURED AND MODERN SHOWING CRYSTAL'S FLEXIBILITY AS A STYLIST

WHAT ARE YOUR FUTURE PLANS?

My goal as a stylist is to support personalities, designers, and magazines in producing high-end quality images. We are more than able to create these images, so making it happen is my biggest goal.

I would love to do more work in Nigeria or other places that need help in building their fashion industry like Senegal or Ghana, working with strong emerging designers to help promote their work on an international level, not just in Africa. I definitely look forward to eventually moving back to Nigeria to share the knowledge I have gained abroad and contribute to developing the fashion industry on the continent and working with magazines, personalities, photographers and designers to create amazing images.

WHICH ACHIEVEMENT ARE YOU MOST PROUD OF?

Publication of my first shoot for *Sublime* magazine was definitely my proudest moment. I am currently working with the NTM Fashion and Design Week (in Nigeria) with strong up and coming designers and helping them create their vision through their designs. This is also a career highlight for me – being able to give something back.

WHO ARE YOUR MAIN CLIENTS?

Anita Quansah (jewellery designer), British Fashion Council -London Fashion Week , NSPCC fundraisers, Elegance (French fashion show), NTM Fashion and Design Week (Nigeria), Nkwo (designer), and music video with Lemar's protégé Effie Effie.

CARMEN
HAID

ww.carmenhaid.com

(ABOVE) CARMEN'S DESIGNS
FOR THE ATELIER-MAYER.COM
GALLERY INSPIRED BY AUSTRIAN
SECESSIONIST JOSEF HOFFMANN,
(RIGHT) A PRIVATE ROOM
INSPIRED BY HER SEAMSTRESS
GRANDMOTHER

Brief Biography

CARMEN STUDIED AT THE LONDON
COLLEGE OF FASHION AND TOOK A
DEGREE IN FASHION MANAGEMENT.
SHE BEGAN HER FASHION CAREER
WORKING IN PR FOR A DECADE THEN
WENT ONTO BECOME A STYLIST. SHE
HAS ENCOUNTERED THE FASHION
INDUSTRY ON SEVERAL LEVELS
AND LEARNT HOW TO USE THIS
INSIGHT TO CREATE HER OWN
BRAND, ATELIER MAYER.

(ABOVE) THE GARDEN INSPIRED
BY JARDIN MAJORELLE IN
MARRAKECH AND (RIGHT)
CARMEN HERSELF

HOW DID YOU GET INVOLVED IN FASHION STYLING?

I've been working in the fashion industry for many, many years and previously as a PR and communications director for luxury brands such as YSL and Céline. I did that for over 10 years and in the meantime worked briefly for British *Vogue* to see how it was on the other side. I had my first child while I was at Céline.

I had already thought I wanted to start my own business, but then I got a call from Tommy Hilfiger to set up the press office for the UK. I thought it would be a good experience to have, certainly different to my previous work.

After two years there I became pregnant with my second child and then three years ago I started Atelier-Mayer.com. My main inspiration behind Atelier-Mayer was my late grandmother. In the 1930s, my grandmother had been a couture tailor who had founded her atelier during the Wiener Werkstätte design movement.

In her later life, I spent many summers at her atelier attending fittings, fashion shows, feeling fabrics and just getting the hang of it.

In Austria at the time you could only study fashion design and not really anything behind the scenes, so I had to go abroad. I lived in Munich for a little while and Italy, then moved to London 14 years ago and studied fashion management part time.

I've been collecting vintage since age of three, and have a lot of fashion designer friends who come to my house to look through my wardrobe. They've reworked vintage clothing into new pieces for the collection. I wanted to do something online because I've been a big fan of net-a-porter and relied on buying my wardrobe essentials from there. It took about two years of research before I started the business three years ago. Since then it's gone from strength to strength. It's been a lot of hard work, but very exciting as well.

We originally started online and then moved into a gallery so that people could visit. This was great as we had a lot of clients, especially for red carpet fittings, so there was now a little more space for that. Our main business is still online, however.

QUALIFICATIONS IN THE FIELD?

After studying at the London College of Fashion I would like to have done an MBA in luxury design management at a university in France, but now that I have children it's a full time job, so maybe another time in another life.

I still very much like the academic part of fashion as I think it's quite important. I don't think you necessarily need to have a formal education, depending on what you do. In PR it's all about contacts. I had a very good mentor in Florence, Paul and the whole PR team at YSL, they are old school fashion PRs and so were good mentors.

But a degree definitely helps as it teaches you, especially in retail, how to talk to people and how to multitask.

ANY TIPS FOR BUDDING STYLISTS?

It is important to get as much experience as you can get. Doing long hours, jobs at weekends, it's going the extra mile and sometimes working overtime for free.

Always be hands-on, if you put in the energy it will come back to you.

Get visual references for photo shoots, for example if you are planning to do a tribute to the late Elizabeth Taylor you will need images. It helps to read books where you could research movies she has been in, what styles to go for, and to look at images to see what she was like. So it is helpful to get ideas from the past and translate them into the present.

Always do the research so you are fully prepared. I had clients who wanted to do a Russian doll shoot, so I needed to research and be fully prepared to go into detail on how they should look, their hairstyles, traditional dresses, etc.

CARMEN'S STYLING FOR FASHION BLOGGER BIP LING FOR THE ATELIER-MAYER MAGAZINE VOL. 1 - IN A VINTAGE BOB MACKIE JACKET AND A 60'S LANVIN SCARF AS BOW

A BEAUTIFUL 70'S INSPIRED LOOK
COMPLETE WITH BEEHIVE HAIR

GIVE US A BRIEF OVERVIEW OF WHAT YOU DO.

My days are always totally different. People will call me up to say they need certain clothes for photo-shoots, so I select the clothes that they need. Sometimes I have clients who need to be dressed for a certain event and I want to make sure they are the best dressed in the room.

I also have clients who want to sell their vintage clothes and I will visit them in their homes. I have to estimate what a garment is worth. Sometimes clients want to sell something to me for say £300 but it may not be possible to resell it at a price that I would need to make money.

You need to know a lot about important collections. There are certain collections from the 90's like a black and white dress that Christy Turlington wore, but the 90's for me aren't really 'vintage' enough for my business.

I have to make a judgement; does it work for my business? And if I get the vintage piece do I make it modern again? Does it need restoration? All these things need to be thought about.

In the 70's they had horrendous length dresses, not full length but below the knee. It's a very difficult length to carry off if you're not tall. So you have to make a decision, will you alter the length?

I styled Alexa Chung for the 2011 Cannes Film Festival for which I altered a vintage wedding dress. It was a full-length gown that I customised to make it look modern, I cropped it and made it into a tulip hip style dress. It was beautiful; you need to make tiny twists and tweaks to make sure its wearable now.

STYLING BY CARMEN FOR LEFT TO RIGHT, A GLAMOROUS RED FLAPPER DRESS, LAYERS OF GOTHIC BLACK LACE AND A LUXURIOUS FUR ENSEMBLE

WHICH ACHIEVEMENTS ARE MOST PROUD OF?

It's a very difficult question, but I would say I'm most proud of the fact I seem to reach people out there who share a similar view of vintage fashion and who appreciate my business product.

I've created a little following, which is starting to increase and become global and that is my biggest achievement. I don't know anybody who has done what I do. It's a heritage brand online, it's luxury vintage, which doesn't just mean expensive but means attention to detail and to the best customer service.

We have just won an award for the best Future 100 entrepreneurs. And last year we won a global fashion award in New York for best emerging retailer and brand. It's nice for people to recognise that I have a business with a big vision of how global it can become.

My biggest wish is to make beautiful vintage clothes accessible in different countries and places where they don't have the access to luxury vintage items, countries such as Lithuania.

I am so surprised by all the clicks and followers we get online. We have increased by 400% this year, so it is exciting to see people like and appreciate our business around the *world*.

WHAT ARE YOUR FUTURE PLANS?

I did a collaboration with a fashion brand in Qatar called Toujouri. So we will be doing an Atelier-Mayer magazine launch there.

I want Atelier-Mayer to be the net-a-porter of vintage fashion. Another huge online success story.

BIKI
JOHN

STYLING BY BIKI JOHN, ON THE LEFT A PREPPY MENSWEAR LOOK COMPLETE WITH CANDY STRIP BLAZER AND (OPPOSITE) AN IMAGE FROM BIKI'S ZULA SHOOT WHICH WAS EXHIBITED IN CANNES

www.bikijohn.com

Brief Biography

BIKI JOHN IS A FASHION STYLIST, WRITER AND BLOGGER BASED IN BOTH BERLIN AND LONDON. BIKI ORIGINALLY WORKED IN THE LEGAL PROFESSION BEFORE HER DOMINANT CREATIVE PERSONALITY LED HER TO EMBARK ON A FASHION CAREER. BIKI'S PORTFOLIO INCLUDES HIGH-FASHION EDITORIALS, COMMERCIAL STYLING AND CELEBRITY STYLING. SHE IS STRONGLY INFLUENCED BY MUSIC AND FILM AND ENJOYS IT WHEN HER WORK ALLOWS HER TO REFLECT THIS. IN PARTICULAR, SHE TAKES GREAT INSPIRATION FROM THE 1920S, 50S, 70S AND 80S. BIKI IS RENOWNED FOR COMBINING LUXURY GARMENTS, QUIRKY STREET WEAR AND VINTAGE PIECES TO PRESENT A UNIQUE, MEMORABLE MODERN TWIST. HER CREATIVE VISION RUNS THE GAMUT FROM MASCULINE TO FEMININE AND FROM VINTAGE TO MODERN. HER VERSATILITY AND HER TALENT FOR MERGING EDGY WITH CLASSIC SET HER APART FROM THE REST. BIKI ALSO CONTRIBUTES HER UNIQUE PERSPECTIVE AND INSIGHT IN A NUMBER OF DIFFERENT CAPACITIES INCLUDING CREATIVE DIRECTION, SHOOT PRODUCTION, CASTING, AND PHOTO EDITING TO NAME A FEW. NOT CONTENT WITH EXPRESSING HER CREATIVE VISION THROUGH STYLING, BIKI ALSO WORKS AS A FASHION WRITER AND HER WORK HAS BEEN PUBLISHED BY BOTH ESTABLISHED PRINT AND ONLINE EDITORIALS

HOW DID YOU GET INTO THE FIELD?

I left the legal profession to embark on a career in fashion. One of the most important things I learned through my legal career was the importance of practical experience. Consequently, I decided to familiarize myself with the areas of fashion I was most interested in by working in those fields. This led me to interning in a fashion press office, working in the cupboards of magazines like *Tatler* and newspapers like *The Guardian* and assisting in a fashion agent's office that represented fashion stylists, photographers, hair and makeup artists. I knew I wanted to focus on a styling career when I worked as a dresser for On and Off (The Doll Company). I was so inspired and motivated by how integral a stylist was to the smooth running of a fashion show.

DID YOU HAVE ANY SPECIFIC QUALIFICATIONS?

I have no official training or qualifications in styling. My training came from real-life experiences which I got by immersing myself in the field by working in jobs like assisting top international stylists like Hector Castro and interning for high-readership fashion magazines like *InStyle*.

As well as being a stylist, I am also a writer and took a writing course at Central St Martin's to improve my fashion writing technique.

(LEFT) FASHION ROAD KILL IN 'THE MORNING AFTER' SHOOT FOR *PUSH IT MAGAZINE*, (BELOW) FUTURISTIC GLAMOUR FOR PORTUGUESE MAGAZINE *ZOOT*. (RIGHT) EYE CATCHING MENSWEAR - MIXING CASUAL TROUSERS AND TRAINERS WITH A JAZZY TRILBY AND TAILORED WAISTCOAT

ANY TIPS FOR BUDDING STYLISTS?

The tips I have come from my own personal experience and they are mainly: When one wants to embark on a fashion stylist career, they must be prepared to face the fact that a lot of assisting and interning jobs are unpaid. Therefore, they must assess and evaluate their finances first and make sure they have a source of reliable and regular income to support them during the beginning stages of their stylist career.

I believe that all budding stylists should join the website Whoistesting.com. Whoistesting.com is a London-based site dedicated to fashion and beauty photographers, stylists, and hair and makeup artists from around the UK and worldwide who are actively testing. Having had no official stylist training, qualifications or contacts when I began styling, this site helped me meet a community of like-minded people and my first test with a photographer on this site landed me my first front cover and published work, and the rest as they say is history.

As good and beneficial as fashion schools may be, I cannot over stress the importance of learning on the job when it comes to styling. So I would advise all budding stylists to assist top stylists as well as styling on their own test shoots. Personally, I feel that is the best way to network, learn how to work in a team and hone your craft.

BRIEF OVERVIEW OF WHAT YOU DO?

Presently I work as a fashion stylist, writer and blogger. This means that one day is never the same as the next and this is what I find so fulfilling about my career. So for example one day I can be running around a city prepping for a shoot and then going to a studio for a model casting and the next I can be writing a review on a designer's collection, whilst simultaneously writing a commercial newsletter for a PR company. I recently started my own blog - myfashionslashlife.wordpress.com - which allows me to write about the topics in fashion and beauty that inspire me and that I feel can be a source of guidance for people.

**ANOTHER ECLECTIC OUTFIT
AND HAIR PIECE**

(LEFT) A BLACK AND WHITE
FASHION FOR THE FASHPACK
BLOG AND (RIGHT) BIKI'S
FASHION WEEK ACCESS PASS

WHAT ACHIEVEMENT ARE YOU MOST PROUD OF?

I styled a fashion editorial, which was shot by the very talented photographer, Marcelo Benfield. He later entered the editorial for the Cannes photo mode, '8ème Festival International de la Photographie de Mode' in 2010; and our image ended up being selected for the exhibition.

WHO ARE YOUR MAIN CLIENTS?

Commercial clients include: Premium Exhibitions, F95 The Fashion Store, Lipsy, Ray Ban, MyAsho.com

Personalities I've styled include: VV Brown (singer), Angellica Bell (TV presenter) and The Do Band (music group)

Publications worked for: *Zoot, Arise, Clash, Andmen, OE, Blink, Sublime, Husk,* Mercedes Benz Fashion Week magazine (Berlin) and *Push It.*

WHAT ARE YOUR FUTURE PLANS?

I am particularly excited about two upcoming projects- one is a children's short stories book I am writing which is aimed at children from the ages of seven to twelve. For this book, I am collaborating with a top fashion illustrator who will bring my short tales of magic and adventure to visual life. My aim is for the book to be inspirational and aspirational for children and I am thoroughly enjoying working on a project that will fuse creativity in both the written and visual sense.

One of the reasons I embarked on a fashion career was to showcase the talents of the African community both directly (for e.g. promoting the collection of an emerging African designer) and indirectly (for e.g. highlighting civilians (non-industry people) who have been influenced by African tradition). This is why I have joined as in-house stylist for a site called Stylecasted.com (www.stylecasted.com). Stylecasted is a digital on-going global exploration of African style heritage and its myriad of reflections.

FARAH
KABIR

www.dresscodebyfarah.com

(ABOVE) JEWELLERY STYLING
FOR HAYA MBC MAGAZINE
AND (RIGHT) FARAH HERSELF
IN HER OFFICES

Brief Biography

FARAH KABIR, HAS AN INTERNATIONAL
HERITAGE, A BELGIAN CITIZEN
ADOPTED BY PARENTS OF
MOROCCAN DESCENT. SHE TRAINED
AS AN IMAGE CONSULTANT IN PARIS
AND DID A FASHION STYLING COURSE
WITH THE LONDON COLLEGE OF
FASHION. SHE LIVED IN BELGIUM UNTIL
2003 AND STUDIED PUBLIC RELATIONS
IN BRUSSELS BEFORE MOVING TO
DUBAI WHERE SHE STILL RESIDES.

AS A LITTLE GIRL FARAH ALWAYS
LOVED DRESSING UP AND SHOPPING
AND USED TO CREATE CLOTHES FOR
HER BARBIE DOLLS AS SHE WAS NEVER
SATISFIED WITH THE OUTFITS THEY
CAME WITH.

SHOOTS FOR (TOP) *BROWNBOOK*
AND (BOTTOM) *FRIDAY*
MAGAZINES

HOW DID YOU GET INTO THE FIELD?

At the age of 25, I had quit my second modelling agency job. I have worked in two modelling agencies as manager. I didn't know what I wanted to do, but was pretty sure I did not want to go back to an agency, but only offers from agency were coming. I ended up working for a while in a very avant-garde boutique selling designers like Demeulemeester, Yamamoto, Comme des Garçons. I really loved dressing up people and learning all about the creators, but something was still lacking. One day a stylist came in scouting the store, I took her around and we ended fitting her for 3 hours. She told me that I had a real talent, that I should be a stylist and that the company she was working for was recruiting. I did not know much about the field and the job sounded like a big joke or a big dream; shopping for a living (at the time to dress TV presenters) sounded unreal. I had nothing to lose, went for the 3-day test and got the job. That's how my story started.

ANY TIPS FOR BUDDING STYLISTS?

Try the unexpected, explore and be creative. Show your creativity and your personality in your work.

Always have an open mind, be curious, explore, and ask questions about everything.

Research is a very important part of our work, know your fashion history and style, but also look into what different continents, eras and cultures have to offer.

Be in the moment so that you can capture what your surroundings and nature are offering you. Anything can inspire you, keep your eyes open and listen to the world.

If possible, travel the world; it is so inspiring to do so.

BRIEF OVERVIEW OF WHAT YOU DO

Producing, directing and styling magazine fashion shoots. Styling on TV, still shoots, catalogues, fashion show styling, wardrobe styling on movies and productions, outfit creation for events. Dressing public personalities, image consultancy and personal shopping for clients.

WHAT ACHIEVEMENTS ARE YOU MOST PROUD OF?

My first fashion show was styling for Harvey Nichols and after that, they made me the official stylist for all their trunk and seasonal shows, catalogues and campaigns.

Working on big Hollywood movies (because of a confidentiality contract I unfortunately cannot reveal the names).

Making a difference in people's life by showing them their own beauty and healing their lack of confidence.

Successfully training fellow stylists who now have their own beautiful careers and live off their passion.

FARAH'S PORTFOLIO IS VARIED RANGING FROM SURREALIST INSPIRED STILL LIFE ACCESSORY SHOOTS, TRADITION ARABIAN STYLING AND MILITARY-INSPIRED COMMERCIAL FASHION FOR *FRIDAY* **AND** *ALPHA* **MAGAZINES**

WHO ARE YOUR MAIN CLIENTS?

Socialites and public personalities of
the region, photo studios, production
companies, agencies and local magazines
are my main clients, through them I
have worked with all possible brands and
for clients such as Tag Heuer, Harvey
Nichols, Cartier, DeBeers, Nike, and
many, many more.

WHAT ARE YOUR FUTURE PLANS?

I am currently in the process of opening
my own fashion consultancy firm
offering services in image consulting,
personal shopping, fashion and wardrobe
styling. In the near future, we will have
all services under one roof, hair, makeup,
wardrobe and a tailoring service so that
we are able to cater for everyone.

Another exciting project on my
agenda is to produce the first English
language makeover show created in the
Middle East.

ELAUAN LEE

www.eluan.com

ELAUAN'S CONTROVERSIAL
JEWISH SHOOT

Home Sweet Home

Brief Biography

ELAUAN LEE WAS BORN IN BRIGHTON; SHE GREW UP IN SOMERSET AND STUDIED AT UNIVERSITY COLLEGE OF THE CREATIVE ARTS IN EPSOM. HER DEGREE WAS IN GRAPHIC DESIGN AND SHE TOOK IT IN A CONCEPTUAL DIRECTION. AFTER GRADUATING SHE WENT TO WORK AT *ATTITUDE* MAGAZINE, AND FIVE YEARS LATER SHE IS NOW THE FASHION EDITOR. SHE IS ALSO A FREELANCE STYLIST AND ART DIRECTOR HAVING WORKED ON LONDON FASHION WEEK SHOWS AND RECENTLY WORKED ON *LOADED* MAGAZINE AS THE FASHION EDITOR EXPLORING ANOTHER AREA OF THE MEN'S MAGAZINE SECTOR.

DANIEL RADCLIFFE AS STYLED
BY ELAUAN FOR AN *ATTITUDE*
MAGAZINE COVER SHOOT

'A degree in styling isn't
necessary, just do it'

COULD YOU GIVE US A BRIEF OVERVIEW OF WHAT YOU DO?

Elauan styles menswear for *Attitude*
magazine and also art directs and
produces shoots as well as editing the
fashion pages. These shoots often involve
styling high profile celebrities (not always
men) for the cover. *Attitude* is a lifestyle
and fashion magazine and it's fashion is
extremely well respected reaching one
of the largest men's magazine audiences
in Britain and the best UK selling gay
magazine with huge cover stars such
as Madonna, Kylie Minogue, David
Beckham, and even David Cameron it
has an opinion and intelligence and its
own voice. Attitude is where the cream
of international celebrity goes to talk to
their huge gay audience. When Attitude
began over 18 years ago it was unheard
of for mainstream celebrities to give
interviews to gay magazines. Attitude has
single-handedly changed this and is now
regarded as one of the most important
magazines for celebrities to appear in.

Her freelance work, involves and music
video styling and fashion show art
direction. Most memorably working
with Christopher Shannon Menswear
Spring/Summer 2012 show in September
2011 which was extremely successful
and Elauan's casting was particularly
popular. One of her models, Todd Taylor,
was sought after by several modelling
agencies including some in New York. He
then went on to sign with Models One
and opened the Autumn/Winter 2012
DSquared show in NYC after
being discovered by Elauan.

Fashion styling allows extensive travel.
In no other job would you experience
places such as – Brazil, New York, Italy,
Austria, Maldives, Milan, South Africa
and of course, Paris.

(ABOVE) ELAUAN'S MENSWEAR
STYLING AND (LEFT) A BEHIND THE
SCENES GLIMPSE OF ELAUAN STYLING
A SUMMER SHORTS FEATURE

ELAUAN ON SET WITH THE MALE
MODELS RESTING ON A PROP
CAR, (BELOW) A SHOT FROM THE
FINAL FASHION SPREAD

HOW DID YOU GET INTO THE FIELD?

In 2007 she met Luke Day at a party, the Fashion Editor of *Attitude* magazine, he was dressed as a pirate; she was dressed in an 80's jumpsuit at a mutual friend's house. The friend, Cassie Fitzpatrick, recommended her to for the role of his assistant, and she was called in for an interview. After 5 minutes in the interview room she was offered the job and Luke had been searching through possible candidates for months. He is now fashion Editor at *GQ Style*.

WHAT IS YOUR PROUDEST ACHIEVEMENT?

There was a controversial shoot with a Jewish theme. I got a lot of heat from the Editor and the night before the deadline he pulled it from the issue and I was devastated. To have any chance of being printed he instructed me to find a gay Jewish Rabbi to approve the shoot. I managed to find one and he was cool with it: he just sent me back some styling tips When it came out I had a huge reaction from readers, fellow stylists and industry people all applauding it. It was brave and I loved it.

In early 2012, *Attitude* did a cover shoot with Harry Potter actor Daniel Radcliffe as he launched his career into more serious acting. The shoot in New York is one of Elauan's favourite shoots and Daniel was one of the loveliest celebrities she has ever worked with.

WHAT ARE YOUR FUTURE PLANS?

Elauan can now see herself moving to New York in the next few years to work on a magazine or as a freelance menswear stylist in the American menswear market. Her eventual ambition is to be Art Director of her own company.

ZOE LEM

www.zoelem.co.uk

Brief Biography

A STYLIST AND BOUTIQUE OWNER,
ZOE IS KNOWN FOR HER TELEVISION
WORK WITH TRINNY AND SUSANNAH,
BUT HAS ALSO WORKED IN MUSIC
VIDEO STYLING AND MAGAZINE
PUBLISHING. SHE IS INTERESTED IN
VINTAGE FASHION AND OWNS
A VINTAGE STORE CALLED MY
SUGARLAND. SHE IS LAUNCHING
HER OWN FASHION LABEL BASED ON
VINTAGE-INSPIRED DESIGNS. ZOE
ALSO HOPES TO ESTABLISH A STYLE
ACADEMY TO TEACH PEOPLE HOW
TO BE STYLISTS AND AS A PERSONAL
STYLIST, TO TEACH PEOPLE HOW TO
USE COLOUR AND SHAPE.

BEAUTIFUL VINTAGE STYLE
DRESSES BY ZOE LEM. (FAR LEFT)
PINK FEATHERY DRESS INSPIRED BY
THE 20s AND (LEFT AND BELOW)
BRIDAL WEAR INSPIRED BY THE 30s

HOW DID YOU GET INTO THE FIELD?

Upon graduating with a degree in fashion design and marketing, her first job was in marketing for the fashion council. After eight months she began taking part in test shoots and taking on the odd styling job. Her tests built into a portfolio and she made friends with makeup artists along the way. She then got her first magazine job with Emap setting up the fashion and beauty department for *Big! Magazine* with Kate Finnigan, who then went on to work at *Stella*. She started freelancing and left Emap to concentrate on this full-time. Going on to work with pop stars of the 1990's including Steps and Peter Andre, Zoe liked to mix her workload as a freelancer, covering fashion, music, TV and celebrities. She signed up with an agency that got her TV work with GMTV, The One Show and Trinny and Susannah and she worked with them for 5 years of her career. She has worked on commercials for products such as Nescafé and music promotional videos.

ANY TIPS FOR BUDDING STYLISTS?

Zoe found her degree very helpful for the business angle of working freelance.

A novice stylist should know how clothes are constructed and understand how they move even if they can't sew.

Try not to work just with celebrities, have an interest in clothes and what's on the catwalks, try to have an edge and be inspired by art, fabric, texture and street style – how clothes look on real women.

Gain experience assisting a stylist and dealing with PR people and shop assistants. Interacting with other people well is important, if PRs are unhelpful turn to shops and department stores.

Clothing affects peoples' moods; it makes them feel good. When taking bookings, make sure you understand the brief and fulfil it. Your style should vary from job to job, be open and flexible. As everyone needs to be dressed, be open-minded about who you work with. Zoe has worked with Sheiks among others. Be creative and excited.

WHO ARE YOUR MAIN CLIENTS AND PUBLICATIONS?

BBC, Trinny and Susannah, *Tank*, BT, Scottish Widows, Hair for L'Oreal, Toni and Guy, Andrew Barton, Vidal Sassoon and Saks, Diana Vickers, sent vintage to Adele, *Big! Magazine*, Anneka's Challenge, Robbie Williams – Escapology, Trisha Goddard, vintage for The One Show. Myleene Klass for the *Glamour* Awards, Fearne Cotton, Cat Deeley, Esther Rantzen, French bridal magazines, mainstream catalogues - both commercial and cutting edge.

(FAR LEFT) A BEAUTIFUL 40s ENSEMBLE COMPLETE WITH PARASOL, (LEFT) 1950s INSPIRED LACE DRESS WITH SEQUINED CAPE AND (RIGHT) BEAUTIFUL 40s LACE

ARIETA
MUJAY

@ArietaWHO

(LEFT) ARIETA'S STYLING FOR
RIVER ISLAND'S LUXE SPORTSWEAR
COLLABORATION WITH ADIDAS,
(RIGHT) PACHA'S SUMMER
FASHION COLLECTION FOR
RIVER ISLAND

Brief Biography

ARIETA IS THE UK PR MANAGER FOR
RIVER ISLAND AND HAS WORKED WITH
KELLY ROWLAND AND ALESHA DIXON
FOR THE PRINCE'S TRUST AND WITH
SUPERMODEL ALEK WEK, LILY ALLEN,
WALE ODEM TO NAME BUT A FEW
OF HER CLIENTS. SHE ALSO HAS A
COLUMN FOR AFRICAN WEEKLY
MAGAZINE *ALLURE*.

HOW DID YOU GET INTO THE FIELD?

I always wanted to work in fashion, but I'm a business graduate. I have two degrees: Business Marketing and Business Law. When I was at university in Brighton I helped a friend of mine, who liked my style, with a final year project. I just took people saying to me "ooh you look nice" a bit more forward into a potential career.

I met Didi Danso when she worked at the *Daily Mirror*; she was the first person to give me an opportunity by letting me assist her on a shoot. I worked for free for two years, very hard work but I loved it.

I'm purely focused on Africa and bringing African fashion to the forefront. I want to show people there is a lot more to African fashion than just the fabric. I take time out of my day job and use my holiday time to fly to Africa.

QUALIFICATIONS IN FIELD?

I have experience. And as we all know fashion is not what you know, it's who you know, darling!

MORE FROM THE ADIDAS SPRING
SUMMER 2012 COLLECTION

DO YOU HAVE ANY TIPS FOR BUDDING STYLISTS?

Give yourself loads of time. You have to intern; you have to assist for free. I had a 40-hour per week job, which I did in two days.

I interned for two years. A lot of people think it's quite easy to work in this industry, but I say go and work for free then get to back to me! I get involved with brands.

You have to do what you love otherwise there is no point. And you have to know your target market.

WHAT ACHIEVEMENT ARE YOU MOST PROUD OF?

Working on fashion weeks in Africa. South African fashion week has only been going for four years so it is exciting to watch the growth of the industry in Africa. I'm incredibly proud that I'm part of it.

CLIENTS AND PUBLICATIONS WORKED FOR?

Fashionista, River Island PR, rod.com, *Look* and *Heat*, 'Project Runway' (NY), Brigit Awofika, Deola Sagoe, and African hip-hop artist Sasha P. just to name a few.

WHAT ARE YOUR FUTURE PLANS?

Although I'd like to describe myself as a global ghetto girl, I love street fashion, I love seeing African fashion growing and would love to help African fashion explode internationally.

ARIETA HAS WORKED WITH
SEVERAL CELEBRITIES INCLUDING
(TOP LEFT) PALOMA FAITH,
(BOTTOM LEFT) A SWIMWEAR
SHOT FROM THE PACHA RIVER
ISLAND COLLECTION AND
(ABOVE) THE ADIDAS OLYMPIC
COLLECTION TO CELEBRATE
LONDON 2012

ROSA OSPINA

www.rosaomakeup.com

Brief Biography

I WAS BORN IN LONDON (TO AN ENGLISH MOTHER AND COLOMBIAN FATHER, HENCE THE NAME!), BUT WHEN I WAS EIGHT MY FAMILY MOVED TO THE IRISH COUNTRYSIDE. THE COMMUNITY I GREW UP IN WAS SOMEWHAT LIMITED CREATIVELY AND I STRUGGLED, AS MOST CHILDREN DO, TO FIT INTO THE SOMEWHAT RURAL COMMUNITY. I COULD NEVER FIGHT THE URGE TO DRESS UP IN SOME WILD COSTUME EVERY DAY AND WHEN I BECAME A TEENAGER I CONTINUED TO EXPERIMENT WITH CLOTHES AND MAKEUP AND BRIGHT HAIR COLOURS! MY PARENTS ALWAYS ALLOWED AND ENCOURAGED ME TO PLAY AROUND WITH THESE THINGS, ALTHOUGH THEY WERE NEVER IMPRESSED WITH THE TOWELS COVERED IN PINK HAIR DYE OR NAIL VARNISH ON THE TABLETOPS. I THINK I WAS 16 WHEN I DECIDED I WAS TOO OBSESSED WITH FASHION NOT TO GET INVOLVED IN IT. I HAD TOYED WITH THE IDEA OF BEING A DESIGNER, BUT DECIDED I DIDN'T HAVE THE ORIGINALITY TO SUCCEED! A LIFE LONG INTEREST IN HISTORY MEANT I WAS ALWAYS LOOKING BACKWARDS FOR INSPIRATION AND WOULD NEVER BE "FASHION FORWARD".

DESPITE SOME TIME TOYING WITH OTHER MORE "SERIOUS" PROFESSIONS, I KNEW MY HEART ALWAYS LAY WITH GENERALLY MAKING THINGS BEAUTIFUL! WHEN I FINISHED SCHOOL, WITH GRADES THAT REFLECTED MY LACK OF INTEREST IN ACADEMIA, I DECIDED TO TAKE A GAP YEAR. I HEADED TO BARCELONA FOR A 10-DAY HOLIDAY WITH A FRIEND OF MINE. 10 DAYS, WHICH TURNED INTO 4 WEEKS, WHICH TURNED INTO 4 AND HALF YEARS! I SPENT THAT TIME WORKING WITH THEATRE GROUPS AND PERFORMERS, DOING SHOOTS AND GENERALLY BEING A CONTINENTAL BOHEMIAN! I THEN MOVED BACK TO IRELAND AND NOW I WORK ON A FREELANCE BASIS ALL OVER THE COUNTRY.

AS WELL AS STYLING ROSA ALSO
DOES HAIR AND MAKE-UP,
(TOP LEFT) AN ON SET SHOT FOR
THE FILM, *FACTORY GIRL* AND
(ABOVE) A LIVING DOLL FASHION
SHOOT FOR ALICE HALLIDAY.
BOTH SHOWING OFF ALL THREE
OF HER SKILLS

A SHOOT CONTRASTING AN
ELEGANT LACE DRESS WITH AN
URBAN BACKGROUND AND
(OPPOSITE) IMAGES FROM THE
2011 SHARON ROSE GODDESS
KNITWEAR COLLECTION

HOW DID YOU GET INTO THE FIELD?

Knowing that I needed to start doing what I love, I trawled the want ads for people casting plays. I called a number, told the man on the other end that I was a "makeup artist/hairdresser/wardrobe mistress" and he said, "Great, we open in two weeks". So, I did one play. I got paid €30, we did a 2-week run, and I never had so much fun in my life. From that one show I got a job working for a drag queen and an offer for another show. And so it escalated! I would be given a budget by the director and we would discuss the characters and the story. Then I would spend six weeks running around, sourcing props, working with the set designers on the layout, finding costumes, begging, borrowing and, in one case, actually stealing! Then the show would open, and I would do everyone's hair and makeup. It was honestly the best experience of my life. It taught me so much and really let me cut my teeth in the most fun way possible.

WHAT WERE YOUR QUALIFICATIONS?

I originally planned on doing a styling degree at the London College of Fashion and applied for various costume construction courses, but none of them ever worked out. Everything I know about styling I found out for myself! I did a short course in period hair and makeup after I'd been working in theatre a couple of years; I felt there were gaps in my knowledge that I wanted to fill. But the art of putting things together is innate and I'm not sure it can be taught!

DO YOU HAVE ANY TIPS FOR BUDDING STYLISTS?

Do everything, any job, which is offered to you! Forget about getting paid, just do it! Make your own opportunities, create the image you want, blag your way into work exchanges, don't be afraid to ask designers and shops if you can borrow clothes, and always remind the model to wear nude underwear! They WILL forget.

BRIEF OVER VIEW OF WHAT YOU DO?

I consider myself responsible for the overall appearance of everything I do. I always joke that if I was 6-foot model and had a good camera, I wouldn't need anyone else on a shoot!

At this point in Ireland I am hugely involved with the vintage community. I do shoots and fashion shows, but mainly I work with clients on a one-to-one basis. My average working week can be wild and varied. Recently, in the space of one day, I styled a burlesque dancer, a bride, and a drag queen! It's my job to find the right clothes, shoes, accessories and props, to design the hair and makeup and keep the client happy. Not too hard, right? I'm somewhat of a control freak, everything has to be perfect and I have trouble trusting that other people will make the right decisions!

I have also always been an avid collector of everything. It amazes people how much of the stuff I use comes out of my own house and wardrobe!

WHICH ACHIEVEMENT ARE YOU MOST PROUD OF?

It's hard for me to say. As wet as it sounds, every time I do a job and the client is happy it feels like an achievement! I do, however, remember clearly the first time a show I worked on opened to an audience of 200. That in itself was amazing and I was so elated when I overheard someone in the bathroom saying that the piece looked flawless. It's easy for people not to notice how much work goes into a production like that and it meant so much to me to know someone cared!

PUBLICATIONS YOU'VE WORKED ON?

I've had work in several Irish publications such as *U*, *Prudence*, *Confetti* and *The Irish Time* magazine. Blogs such as 100-layer cake and One Fab Day have also shared shoots of mine. I've had clients appear on The Late Late show and Catalan television.

WHAT ARE YOUR FUTURE PLANS?

I hope one day to run a giant props and wardrobe store! An emporium of wonderful things that people can rent for shoots and productions. Until then I will continue to work freelance and am planning on opening a studio in Dublin soon! Other than that, I simply plan on injecting a little magic into life and perhaps making the world a more beautiful place, for everyone.

BEAUTIFUL, DELICATE IMAGES FROM THE ALICE HALLIDAY FASHION LINE AND (LEFT) AN EASTER THEME ON A PRETTY COUNTRYSIDE SET

HERSHEY PASCUAL

Brief Biography

FASHION STYLIST HERSHEY PASCUAL STARTED HER CAREER ASSISTING AT BRITISH *ELLE* IN 2000. SINCE THEN SHE HAS WORKED FOR PRESTIGIOUS PUBLICATIONS SUCH AS *W, WWD, THE HARRODS MAGAZINE, THE SUNDAY TIMES STYLE, OK!* AND *STAR*. HER CAREER HAS LED HER TO STYLE WELL-KNOWN FACES IN THE FILM, FASHION, TELEVISION AND MUSIC INDUSTRY INCLUDING: JOSEPH FIENNES, RICKY GERVAIS, THE SATURDAYS, MYLEENE KLASS, COLEEN MCLOUGHLIN, STEVE JONES, WESTLIFE, THE WANTED, MCFLY, ALAN CARR, JANICE DICKENSON AND ANNA FRIEL. SHE HAS ALSO REPORTED AND PRESENTED ON TELEVISION SHOWS LIKE ITV'S GMTV, CHANNEL 4'S BIG BROTHER'S LITTLE BROTHER AND HOW TO LOOK GOOD NAKED, BBC ONE'S BLUE PETER, SKY LIVING'S BRITAIN'S NEXT TOP MODEL, SKY NEWS AND CHANNEL 5 NEWS. IN 2012 SHE SET UP FASHION LABEL, SEVILLA BY HERSHEY (WWW.SEVILLABYHERSHEY.COM), A WOMEN'S WEAR HIGH STREET FASHION LINE FOR STYLISH PROFESSIONAL WOMEN.

HOW DID YOU GET INTO THE FIELD?

While studying for a degree in Anthropology at Durham University Hershey did work experience at *Nova*, *Cosmopolitan* and *Marie Claire* as she had always had a personal interest in fashion and an ambition to be involved in magazines. Once she graduated she went on to work at UK *Elle*.

DO YOU HAVE ANY TIPS FOR BUDDING STYLISTS?

There are no set rules for making it in the fashion industry. It's very much a situation of it's not what you know it's whom you know. Determination, creativity, hard work and ambition all will cumulate to success. You have to live and breathe fashion.

(BELOW) HERSHEY STYLING A MODEL IN FEDORA AND TAILORED SHORTS, (RIGHT) A PRETTY KITTEN BOW JUMPSUIT

BRIEF OVERVIEW OF WHAT YOU DO?

I'm Executive Style Editor for celebrity weekly *Star* Magazine. I also work for *OK!* My work involves commissioning, styling photo shoots and writing fashion, beauty and travel pieces. I'm a contributor for Chanel Five News and OK! TV. Other TV shows I've worked for include GMTV, Blue Peter and Big Brother.

WHAT ACHIEVEMENT ARE YOU MOST PROUD OF?

I was a fashion editor at age 23. Looking back, it was a big achievement for being so young. It's great working for successful national publications that are read all over the world. I enjoyed working at Britain's Next Top Model especially when I appeared as a judge with Lisa Snowdon on the fourth series. Other high points include judging for London Fashion Week events with singer VV Brown and designer Luella Bartley.

HERSHEY HAS STYLED MANY CELEBRITIES INCLUDING (BELOW LEFT) WESTLIFE IN THIS RAT PACK INSPIRED SHOT AND (BELOW RIGHT) RICKY GERVAIS AS A BARROW BOY

WHAT ARE YOUR FUTURE PLANS?

I have launched a capsule collection called 'Sevilla by Hershey'. It's a womenswear collection: sexy, smart work and daywear pieces. It includes classic and timeless staple items that are also trend led. I'll be selling it on Asos.com in the boutique section. I'm really excited about my first new fashion line. It seemed like the natural next step from styling, fashion editing and TV reporting.

It's hard work and also rewarding to be working for yourself on something that can develop to be great one day. I'm also writing a chick lit book. It is an easy-to-read fun fiction on dating and relationships in the city.

MAIN CLIENTS?

Other than the magazines she works for, she has styled stars such as Coleen Rooney, Sophie Anderton, The Saturdays, Myleene Klass and Meg Matthews. TV work includes Lorraine, GMTV, Five News and I'm a Celebrity Get Me Out of Here. She also does regional radio pieces.

NIKKI
PENNIE

@nikkipennie

Brief Biography

NIKKI, A NATIVE BRIT NOW BASED IN LOS ANGELES, BEGAN HER FASHION CAREER AFTER OBTAINING A DEGREE IN FASHION MANAGEMENT AT THE LONDON COLLEGE OF FASHION ALMOST A DECADE AGO. SHE THEN WENT ON TO GAIN EXPERIENCE IN PUBLIC RELATIONS FOR EUROPEAN BRANDS SUCH AS LUELLA AND CÉLINE AND THE LONDON FASHION PR AGENCY MODUS PUBLICITY. FOLLOWING THIS SHE WORKED AS DIRECTOR OF PUBLIC RELATIONS AT THE BRITISH FASHION HOUSE, ISSA, FOR SEVERAL YEARS. WHILE THERE, SHE PUT ISSA ON THE MAP AND MADE HEADLINES AND FRONT PAGE NEWS WITH THE CELEBRITIES AND INTERNATIONAL SOCIALITES THAT SHE STYLED FOR THE BRAND INCLUDING THE NEW DUCHESS OF CAMBRIDGE, THE FORMER KATE MIDDLETON. NIKKI INTRODUCED KATE TO ISSA AND CULTIVATED THE RELATIONSHIP; SO MUCH SO THAT IT BECAME A LONG-STANDING RUMOR THAT KATE WAS THE OFFICIAL BRAND AMBASSADOR. NIKKI STYLED KATE IN NUMEROUS OUTFITS OVER THE COURSE OF HER DURATION AT THE BRAND.

NIKKI MADE A JUMP OVER THE ATLANTIC TO LOS ANGELES TWO YEARS AGO. SHE FOCUSED PREDOMINANTLY ON STYLING AND HAS POOLED HER ASSETS AND STRENGTHS TOGETHER TO BECOME LABELLED AS THE "BRIT IT GIRL/STYLIST" BY THE LA TIMES. SHE WORKED WITH A VARIETY OF CELEBRITIES SUCH AS MADONNA, PAULA ABDUL, NICOLE SCHERZINGER, PIPPA MIDDLETON, KALEY CUOCO, AMY POEHLER, JULIE BOWEN, TERI HATCHER, JENNA FISCHER, SHENAE GRIMES, LYNN COLLINS, STEVEN STRAIT, NATURI NAUGHTON, MICHAELA CONLIN, CASSIE SCERBO, JULIA JONES, SCOTT CAAN, GRACE PAK, ALEX O'LOUGHLIN, DANIEL DAE KIM, LINDA CARDELLINI, KHERINGTON PAYNE AND SARA PAXTON. NIKKI HAS FREQUENTLY STYLED SHOOTS WITH THE RENOWNED CELEBRITY PHOTOGRAPHER ART STREIBER. RECENTLY, NIKKI STYLED THE COVER OF *THE HOLLYWOOD REPORTER* OSCAR ROUNDTABLE ISSUE WHICH INCLUDED CHARLIZE THERON, VIOLA DAVIS, CAREY MULLIGAN, MICHELLE WILLIAMS, OCTAVIA SPENCER AND GLENN CLOSE.

NIKKI HAS STYLED FOR VARIOUS MAGAZINES INCLUDING (TOP LEFT) *PEOPLE*, (BOTTOM LEFT) *THE HOLLYWOOD REPORTER* AND (ABOVE) *HARPER'S BAZAAR*

HOW DID YOU GET INTO THE FIELD?

I always wanted to be in fashion from the age that I could walk! My mother is one of the most stylish ladies I know and that inspired me to take a career in fashion seriously. I knew I never wanted to be a designer, but a fashion business woman!

WHAT QUALIFICATIONS DID YOU HAVE?

I did a BA (Hons) Fashion Management at the London College of Fashion and then I went on to work for different designers and companies doing fashion public relations. I was introduced to Daniella Helayel from Issa when she was starting out through my dear friend Carmen Haid. That was an amazing opportunity for me at a young age. I was head of communications there. The predominant part of my job was to dress high profile people in the brand. This became so successful that I started to spend a lot of time here in LA where I now reside. I then left Issa and went into styling full time.

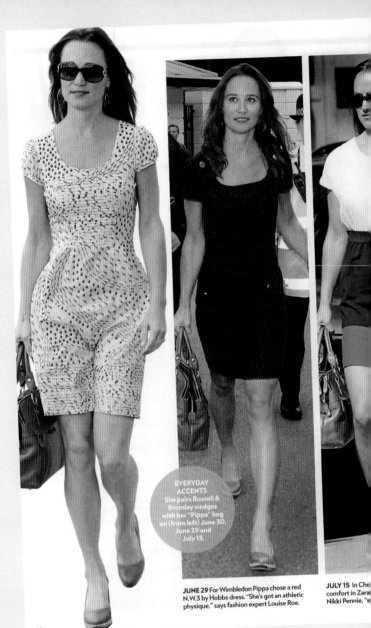

EVERYDAY ACCENTS
She pairs Russell & Bromley wedges with her "Pippa" bag on (from left) June 30, June 29 and July 15.

JUNE 29 For Wimbledon Pippa chose a red N.W.3 by Hobbs dress. "She's got an athletic physique," says fashion expert Louise Roe.

JULY 15 In Che comfort in Zara Nikki Pennie, "

68

AS A BRITISH STYLIST IN THE UNITED STATES, NIKKI HAS BECOME SOMETHING OF AN EXPERT ON SISTERS KATE AND PIPPA MIDDLETON

DO YOU HAVE ANY TIPS FOR BUDDING STYLISTS?

Don't give up!! It's definitely hard work and not as glamorous as it seems, but it's worthwhile and the best part of the job is when you make someone feel like a million dollars!!!

CAN YOU GIVE A BRIEF OVERVIEW OF YOUR WORK?

The key element when you work with celebrities is to collaborate with them on outfits that suit their personality and that they feel most comfortable with. That is the most important factor!

Kate's Sleek Sister

The streets of London serve as a runway for Pippa Middleton! Bold prints and slim-fitting jeans are staples in her fun and feminine wardrobe

MAY 19 Pippa exudes laid-back cool in a sleeveless blouse, 7 for All Mankind jeans and an L.K. Bennett "Annina" bag.

LOOKALIKE SISTERS: Pippa hit the street in May sporting the same Whistles jacket that older sis Kate (top right) wore to lunch with Camilla Parker Bowles in February.

" Pippa will often borrow dresses from Kate. They are the same size . . . and have quite similar tastes"

—KATIE NICHOLL, ROYAL BIOGRAPHER

How She Does It . . .

1 SHE WEARS A DARING PATTERN
"She is not afraid of bold colors or prints," stylist pal Nikki Pennie says of the more risk-taking Middleton sister. "She always gets it right and makes a splash!"

2 SHE FLAUNTS HER LEGS
Fit enough to complete a 50-mile race, Pippa has earned her toned legs and loves to show them off while sporting short hemlines or skinny jeans.

3 SHE HIGHLIGHTS HER WAIST
Whether it's a cropped jacket or a wrap dress, the Pilates devotee smartly accentuates her slim center. "She's not afraid of anything body-conscious," says Alisande Healy Orme, author of *Kate Style*.

WHAT ACHIEVEMENTS ARE YOU MOST PROUD OF?

There have been many recently! I think all of my fashion reporting for CNN and other networks and the Internet is definitely a dream I have fulfilled. Also my Oscar actresses' cover for *The Hollywood Reporter*.

WHAT ARE YOUR PLANS FOR THE FUTURE?

I am focusing on my fashion hosting/ reporting on television, the Internet and all of the YouTube channels that are launching this year! Plus my own YouTube channel: Princess for Pennies.

KALVIN
RYDER

AS A MUSIC INDUSTRY STYLIST,
KALVIN WORKS WITH ARTISTS
SUCH AS KELLY ROWLAND AND
AYLAR TO ENSURE THEY HAVE THE
CORRECT COMMERCIAL IMAGE
FOR THEIR ALBUM COVERS, LIVE
SHOWS AND MUSIC VIDEOS

Brief Biography

KALVIN HAD ALWAYS ADMIRED
HIS HEROES KYLIE MINOGUE AND
STEPS AND THEIR THEATRICAL TOUR
COSTUMES. HE WENT ON TO INTERN
AT RECORD COMPANIES SUCH AS
VIRGIN V2 AFTER DROPPING OUT
OF HIS A-LEVEL COURSES. THIS THEN
LED TO HIS DREAM JOB, STYLING
INTERNATIONAL AND EUROPEAN
MUSIC STARS FOR THEIR UK TOURS
AND VIDEOS.

HOW DID YOU GET INTO THE FIELD?

I started with work experience for record companies when I was 18 years old, initially in the press offices. The first label I worked for was V2, part of Virgin, working with Liberty X and the Stereophonics, on the press side really. Then I moved to different labels and got more involved in the creative side, became a marketing manager and video commissioner. It was as a video commissioner that I started getting involved with styling and the visuals and images of the artists. I was approached by one artist, Cascada. We planned an album with her and I left my job to become the stylist for her UK tour. That was my big break. We had two platinum albums with her and a gold album, several top ten and number one hits. She was really big at that time, one of the biggest dance acts in the world. We went to America with her. It was a pretty exciting period.

DO YOU HAVE ANY TIPS FOR BUDDING STYLISTS?

I think if you want to be involved in styling someone or even as a behind-the-scenes creative you first need to find out what you like, for example the artists you are into and trends you like rather than what is current or hot. Everything runs in a cycle so even if what you like now is not in fashion, it will come into fashion eventually.

Learn about who are you are working with, find out about their team, try and get it to work with that person. Always take an internship over paid work that you aren't that interested in. It can stop you doing what you want to do. So it is better to take an unpaid internship doing something you enjoy, and when your passion is recognized by others you will be on your way. That's what I did.

KALVIN DID A LOT OF WORK
WITH SWEDISH SINGER SONG
WRITER BASSHUNTER, WORKING
ON HIS FIRST ARENA TOUR AND
PERFECTING HIS IMAGE FOR HIS
LAUNCH ONTO THE UK MARKET

BRIEF OVERVIEW OF WHAT YOU DO?

Basically my work is more than just being a general stylist. Usually when I am called in, I oversee the whole campaign from the album artwork and music videos to the live appearances and I make sure everything is consistent and interlinked. I will ensure that the outfits and the whole campaign is right for the artist as a brand and for their market.

WHICH ACHIEVEMENT ARE YOU MOST PROUD OF?

Overseeing the creative elements for Basshunter's first arena tour in 2008 – that was amazing as I got to work out all the outfits, all the visuals and all the merchandise. That was the kind of thing I had always wanted to do when I saw tours of other artists like Kylie Minogue when I was younger. I always thought how terrific that would be to do and I actually got to do it! Seeing all your work coming to life in an arena is fantastic.

WHO ARE YOUR MAIN CLIENTS?

I specialize in the more commercial end of the market. A lot of European acts come to me who are big in Sweden or Germany and are about to embark on a tour of the UK, I will make sure their image is right; artists like Cascada, Basshunter and most recently Alexandra Stan. I work with the Ministry of Sound and on the music videos for a lot of their acts. The biggest client I've probably worked with was Kelly Rowland on her 2011 record 'What a Feeling'. I coordinated the video and all the creative work with her not just on the video, but on all of the promotion surrounding it.

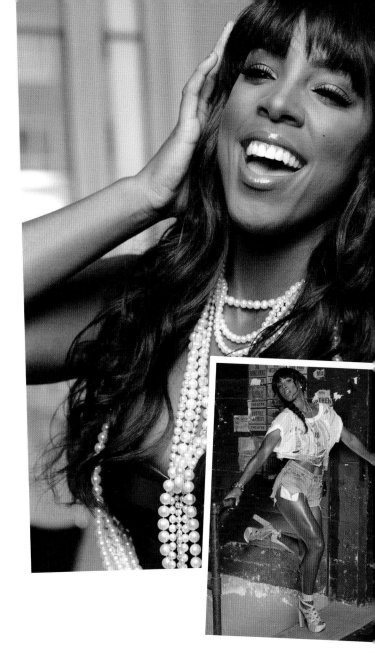

WHAT ARE YOUR FUTURE PLANS?

In 2012 I think I am moving back to LA, I do a lot of work with a director called Alex Helens over in LA and have styled quite a few of his music videos working with people like Kesha and Taio Cruz. So I am going to relocate over there and collaborate with him and see what happens from there. I would love to have a career like William Baker. He was known for all his work with Kylie and was her confidante and key to some of her success before becoming high profile in his own right.

ANGELA SCANLON

www.angelascanlon.com

Brief Biography

ANGELA SCANLON IS A TV PRESENTER, FASHION WRITER AND STYLIST. SHE APPEARS REGULARLY ON IRISH CHANNELS RTE AND TV3 PRESENTING STRANDS ON SHOWS SUCH AS FOUR LIVE, XPOSE, OFF THE RAILS AND TWO TUBE. SHE HAS ALSO INTERVIEWED A LONG LIST OF CELEBRITIES AND LEGENDS INCLUDING CHRISTIAN LOUBOUTIN, BOB GELDOF, ROISIN MURPHY, MARY KATRANTZOU AND KANYE WEST.

HAVING LIVED IN NEW YORK, ASIA AND AUSTRALIA, ANGELA NOW SPLITS HER TIME BETWEEN DUBLIN AND LONDON. ONE THE FRESHEST FACES IN FASHION, ANGELA IS ALWAYS SEEKING OUT THE LATEST UNDERGROUND BANDS, BRANDS AND ARTISTS TO INTERVIEW OR WRITE ABOUT ON HER BLOG.

ANGELA IS A CONTRIBUTING EDITOR FOR *GRAZIA DAILY*, *TATLER*, *THE SUNDAY TIMES STYLE* **MAGAZINE**, *THE SUNDAY INDEPENDENT* **AND IRELAND'S** *U MAGAZINE*, **WHO NAMED HER IN THE TOP 10 BEST-DRESSED IRISH WOMEN. "WALKING WARDROBE", A REGULAR FEATURE IN** *TATLER* **SAW ANGELA MODELLING FOR PHOTO SHOOTS IN THE OUTFITS SHE STYLED.**

ANGELA IS CURRENTLY WORKING ON HER FIRST BOOK DUE FOR RELEASE IN 2012. ANGELA IS ALSO A BRAND CONSULTANT AND HAS WORKED ON CREATIVE PROJECTS FOR BIG NAMES SUCH AS BROWN THOMAS, EBAY, AVIS, DIAGEO, ROXY, MONSOON AND SPECIAL K. SHE IS THE FACE OF A|WEAR TV IN UK AND IRELAND AND IS AN ONLINE PRESENTER FOR TK MAXX.

(LEFT) A FASHION SHOOT
FOR THREAD MAGAZINE AND
(BELOW) A BEAUTIFUL SOFT
FASHION IMAGE SHOWING
THE GENTLER SIDE OF
ANGELA'S STYLING

IN FASHION CLOSE UPS LIKE
THIS ATTENTION TO DETAIL IS
ESSENTIAL, THE INTRICATE RING
AND TOP WORK WELL WITH PLAIN
BLACK OUTFIT

HOW DID YOU GET INTO THE FIELD?

I just kind of fell in to it! I know everyone says it, but it's true. I was working as an agent for two UK designers and selling some of their stuff in a fashion space in Dublin. I volunteered myself to style a shoot for the entire space and it ended up on the front cover of *The Times*. I was hooked! I then began assisting and one thing led to another.

WHAT WERE YOUR QUALIFICATIONS?

I studied business in university with the intention of eventually opening my own boutique, but somehow ended up hating that idea. For me the best education is in doing; learning on the ground and seeing how it all works. For many, the idea of styling is glamorous and easy, often once people see the work involved it's less appealing!!

ANY TIPS FOR BUDDING STYLISTS?

I don't think you can learn how to work by sitting in a classroom. You've got to get stuck in and see if you can handle it in reality. Put yourself out there; find your own way of doing things and work hard. That's the most important thing. The people who I greatly admire are not lucky or privileged; they are grafters and have earned the respect of everyone they work with by doing just that, working their asses off. There is no other way to have a lasting career.

THESE STREET-STYLE IMAGES SHOW
THE RANGE OF SETTINGS THAT
MIGHT BE APPROPRIATE FOR
A SHOOT

BRIEF OVERVIEW OF WHAT YOU DO?

It really depends on the day! I'm lucky in that I can do a wider variety of things. For me it's important to be challenged constantly as I get bored easily and can't stand repetition. I could be working closely with a brand to develop a strategy or come up with a campaign idea, I may be prepping for an editorial shoot, or filming somewhere, interviewing Christian Louboutin for a magazine or newspaper, or hosting a live event. Every day is different; it keeps me on my toes!

WHICH ACHIEVEMENT ARE YOU MOST PROUD OF?

Being commissioned to write a book. It's something I've always wanted to do and having a team that accept my vision of it completely has been pretty amazing. It's been the most relentless and difficult project I've ever done, but it's been worth it! I can't wait for people to see the result. The blood, sweat and tears will be justified when I see it on the shelves.

WHO ARE YOUR MAIN CLIENTS AND WHICH PUBLICATIONS HAVE YOU'VE WORKED WITH?

Brown Thomas, Topshop, COS, TK Maxx, Vodafone

Publications: *The Sunday Times Style, Tatler, Grazia, The Irish Times, THREAD, U Magazine, The Irish Independent, Le Cool, Totally Dublin LIFE Magazine, MODO, IF Magazine*

WHAT ARE YOUR FUTURE PLANS?

My book launch next year will be huge and I'm also working on a TV show, which is really exciting. None of this Gok Wan naked stuff, real fashion for real women. Style is about so much more than grand statements. I want to connect with women in a way that's authentic and honest, and fun!

COURTNEY
SMITH

@CocoSmithStyle
www.courtneysmith.ie

Brief Biography

COURTNEY SMITH (OR COCO AS HER FASHION FRIENDS CALL HER) IS ADMITTEDLY A FASHION JUNKIE! WITH A COLLECTION OF VINTAGE _VOGUES_ THREATENING TO TAKE OVER HER STUDIO AND A WARDROBE BURSTING WITH MUCH-LOVED STYLISH TREASURES – IT'S NO WONDER SHE FOLLOWED A CAREER PATH INTO FASHION! ALTHOUGH CURRENTLY BASED IN DUBLIN, HER WORK HAS TAKEN HER TO LONDON, MIAMI, NEW YORK, CAPE TOWN AND PARIS.

SLEEK FASHION IMAGES SHOT ON THE ROOF OF THE 18TH CENTURY CUSTOM HOUSE BUILDING IN DUBLIN, AFTER CLIMBING A VERY RICKETY LADDER

CLEVER USE OF REFLECTION TO
GIVE AN ALL ROUND VIEW

WHAT QUALIFICATIONS DID YOU HAVE?

After graduating in fashion design in Dublin, an art history tutor advised Courtney to pursue fashion styling as it was clear that with her lack of patience and preference for the finished product rather than the process of getting there, styling would be a more suitable field for her.

Courtney continued on to complete a post-graduate program in Fashion Styling and Media at the prestigious London College of Fashion.

Although she studied her craft, Courtney insists editorial or creative fashion styling is something that can't really be taught. It's about ideas, individuality, pushing the boundaries to create something new, and of course a vision. Creativity in meeting all styling needs.

HOW DID YOU GET INTO THE FIELD?

At 7 years old she was caught cutting up her mum's clothes to create what she called 'art'. That was when her parents noticed a creative flair in their daughter.

After spending her adolescent years telling her family how to dress before they were allowed leave the house; it seemed only natural to pursue a field in fashion.

ANY TIPS FOR BUDDING STYLISTS?

Work you're little butts off ... and if that fails, work harder!

BRIEF OVERVIEW OF WHAT YOU DO?

She strongly believes in the power of collaboration and has worked on a vast majority of her shoots in partnership with photographer Daniel Holfeld. Over the past four years their shared vision has enabled them to cover a commercial brief while at the same time fulfil a creative vision with strong and vivid imagery.

WHICH ACHIEVEMENT ARE YOU MOST PROUD OF?

She was once almost arrested in Cape Town for trespassing to get the "perfect shot" at a private national park... insisting that nothing will get in the way between her and her finished product!

MAIN CLIENTS AND PUBLICATIONS?

Hello! Skinny Jeans, TV3 Fashion Contributor on 'Xpose' and 'Ireland AM' shows, BT2, Brown Thomas, Penneys (Primark), River Island, Fran & Jane

Publications: *Sunday Times Style, GQ South Africa, The Fashionisto, U magazine, The Sunday Independent Life Magazine, The Irish Independent Weekend, Social & Personal, None Magazine*

WHAT ARE YOUR FUTURE PLANS?

Courtney is currently working on the new spring/summer collection campaigns for a variety of brands and is planning some foreign locations for some exciting new shoots.

(LEFT) SWIMWEAR SHOOT AT A PUBLIC POOL IN CAPE TOWN, MUCH TO THE AMUSEMENT OF LOCAL CHILDREN, (TOP RIGHT) BEACH FASHION, AND (BOTTOM RIGHT) A DOPPELGANGER POSE - HOW OWNERS LOOK LIKE THEIR DOGS

CHIARA
SOLLOA

www.chiaramoda.com

Brief Biography

A LEADING FASHION STYLIST AND COSTUME DESIGNER BASED OUT OF MIAMI, FLORIDA—CHIARA SOLLOA IS A RISING STAR HIGHLY SOUGHT AFTER BY TOP MODELS, SPORTS ICONS AND JET-SETTING CELEBRITIES WHO WANT TO MAKE THEIR MARK. FROM TOP MUSIC PRODUCERS LIKE TIMBALAND, WORLD-RENOWN ARTISTS LIKE RICKY MARTIN, RICK ROSS, PITBULL, YMCMB, AKON AND ALICIA KEYS TO RESPECTED BRAND COMPANIES SUCH AS PUMA, NIKE, VISA, MCDONALDS, BACARDI AND PEPSI—CHIARA IS CELEBRATED FOR HER UNIQUE SENSE OF PERCEPTION AND HER UNCANNY ABILITY OF BRINGING CONSCIOUSNESS TO THE CREATIVE VISION SOUGHT BY HER CLIENTS.

(BOTTOM LEFT) CHIARA HERSELF
(BOTTOM RIGHT) A FASHION
SHOOT IN THE JAMAICAN
BLUE MOUNTAINS

BY THE AGE OF 21, CHIARA'S STRONG WORK ETHIC AND CREATIVE TALENTS EVENTUALLY LED THE WAY TO A POSITION AS A FASHION EDITOR FOR THE MAGAZINE *MAXIM EN ESPAÑOL*. WHILE ATTENDING FASHION SHOWS IN NEW YORK, SHE WAS APPROACHED BY A PRODUCER FOR A TV PROJECT IN MIAMI AND OFFERED A CHANCE TO HOST A SHOW CALLED REEL2REAL. THE EXPOSURE FROM THE SHOW

CHIARA STYLING ON SET

INTRODUCED HER TO MANY FASHION HOUSES THAT SPONSORED THE SHOW. THIS LED TO HER FALLING IN LOVE WITH FASHION AND A TRANSITION TO BEING BEHIND THE CAMERA AS A FASHION STYLIST. HER EXPERIENCE INTERVIEWING CELEBRITIES MADE IT VERY EASY AND COMFORTABLE TO BUILD AN HONEST RELATIONSHIP WITH HER CLIENTS.

From there Chiara branched out as co-founder of her own fashion company providing imaging, consulting and artist development for a long list of clients that included actors, musicians, recording labels, advertising firms, clothing companies and athletes. Through her work Chiara has had the opportunity to work with top directors such as Wayne Isham, Little X, Gil Green, Dean Karr and Malcolm Jones. Chiara quickly found herself immersed in projects from New York to Los Angeles. Today, most of Chiara's work is easily recognizable on network channels including BET and MTV.

Now with over 12 years of experience in the entertainment and marketing industry, Chiara credits most of her inspiration to her family upbringing: her grandmother worked as a wedding gown designer and her uncles were Master Tailors. Chiara was born into fashion. Chiara is as versatile and sophisticated as she is talented. She is currently expanding her work onto the international scene from South America to Asia. In the last year, Chiara spend several months in the fashion capitols of Paris and Tokyo studying fashion trends and styles.

HOW DID YOU GET INTO THE FIELD?

I started as a teen model, which was my first exposure to the business. In college I took a job at a make up counter. I thought I paint and I figured, I can do this—and it beats making lattes. I began doing photo shoots and realized my passion was in fashion. I asked photographers for a chance and began styling test shoots. I worked for a long time for free to create my portfolio and build my name. I have never interned or assisted and learned my rights and wrongs myself, it's been a journey.

WHAT ARE YOUR QUALIFICATIONS?

My experience in art, make up and hair styling helps me to bring my vision clearly to life when I explain to a client what I have in mind.

I also have experience with studying and predicting trends.

I have Haute Couture sewing skills and I can knit. I custom make many pieces for my clients. I also speak Spanish, Italian and Swedish.

DO YOU HAVE ANY TIPS FOR BUDDING STYLISTS?

If you can get a mentor, that's the way to go; assist, watch and learn. Don't be afraid ask, be sincere about your passion.

Do lots of research from magazines, books and films, music, fashion eras and photographers. Fashion is a lifestyle. This will help you to identify and make reference to your vision.

Take care of your credit and learn some accounting skills. You need to have credit cards to shop.

FURTHER BEAUTIFUL IMAGES OF A JAMAICAN MODEL STYLED BY CHIARA ON A FASHION SHOOT IN THE BLUE MOUNTAINS

COULD YOU GIVE US A BRIEF OVERVIEW OF WHAT YOU DO?

Before any of the shopping starts, I identify my clients' needs and put together a presentation by creating a mood board. My boards help my client to visualize what I have in mind from color palette to fabric texture. Then I head out to shop or I have things made. Once I have my looks all set up, I do a fitting and then our shoot takes place and we finish the job off with returns.

WHICH ACHIEVEMENT ARE YOU MOST PROUD OF?

I am most proud of being a fashion pioneer here in Miami. People obviously recognize NYC and LA, but Miami is the future. In Miami there is a handful of us and I am very proud to be amongst the top fashion stylists working full time at what I love to do.

A GOAT JOINS THE FASHION
SHOOT IN JAMAICA AND
(BELOW) A HAREM COSTUME
FOR WISIN Y YANDEL " ZUN ZUN"
MUSIC VIDEO DIRECTED BY
JESSE TERRERO

WHO ARE YOUR MAIN CLIENTS?

305Films, MTV , BET, VH1, Latin Grammys, YMCMB, Nike, Puma, Bacardi, Coors, EA Sports, VISA, Reebok, Dr Pepper, Pepsi, Ford, C&A Clothing , Belks, AKON, Timbaland, Drake, Sean Kingston, Pitbull, Birdman, Alicia Keys, Crisette Michelle, Shania Twain, and the list goes on...

Publications worked for: My work consists more of commercials and video but here are a few. *Glamour, Hello, Loft, OK , Redbook, Ocean Drive, Maxim, Portland Magazine*

WHAT ARE YOUR FUTURE PLANS?

I'm starring in a new reality show for MTV featuring 305films and all the music videos we work on and the drama we encounter. I'm also on the board of directors for a new modelling agency in Miami and NY that focuses more on personally developing models through a boot camp and seminars. Another project is the development of a fashion lifestyle brand with a focus on travel apparel.

133

ALEXIA SOMERVILLE

www.alexiasomerville.com

Brief Biography

ALEXIA SOMERVILLE GRADUATED IN 1997 WITH A BA IN GRAPHIC AND MEDIA DESIGN FROM THE LONDON COLLEGE OF PRINTING WITH A PRIMARY FOCUS ON PHOTOGRAPHY AND ART DIRECTION. SHE SET UP A SMALL DESIGN CONSULTANCY WITH A FRIEND FROM ST. MARTINS, WHO LATER ENCOURAGED HER TO BECOME A STYLIST. THROUGH AN AGENT SHE STARTED DRESSING THE MODELS BACKSTAGE ON MOST OF THE MAIN LONDON FASHION WEEK SHOWS IN 1999 AND THROUGH VARIOUS CONNECTIONS IN LONDON AND PARIS SHE STARTED SHOOTING THE VISUAL STORIES SHE WANTED TO SEE IN PRINT. SHE WAS INTRODUCED TO PHOTOGRAPHER NICK KNIGHT BY HER FRIEND LIBERTY ROSS, WHO HAD BEEN ASKED BY BRITISH *VOGUE* TO CO-ORDINATE A TEAM TO SHOOT A STORY ON LIBERTY. ALEXIA WAS ASKED TO WORK ON THIS PROJECT WITH NICK, ENTITLED 'FORBIDDEN FRUIT' WHICH WAS TO EMBODY THE DELICATE BEAUTY AND SEXUAL UNDERTONES OF FRUITS, FLOWERS AND OF LIBERTY HERSELF.

LATER, SHE WAS COMMISSIONED BY ISABELLA BLOW TO DO A SUPER DELUXE SPORTSWEAR STORY FOR *TATLER*. SINCE THEN SHE HAS DONE NUMEROUS EDITORIAL SHOOTS FOR FASHION/STYLE PUBLICATIONS AROUND THE WORLD (UK, US, FRANCE, SPAIN, SWEDEN, JAPAN, ARAB EMIRATES, AUSTRALIA AND NEW ZEALAND) NOT TO MENTION HER COMMERCIAL ADVERTISING CLIENTS WHO HAVE RANGED FROM OLAY, L'OREAL AND PRETTY POLLY TO VAUXHALL TIGRA, AZUMIT YACHTS, LUX SHAMPOO WITH RACHEL WEISZ AND DULUX AND LUCOZADE TO NAME BUT A FEW. SHE HAS ALSO BEEN BOOKED AS A GUEST SPEAKER ON THE TOPICS SURROUNDING STYLE AT THE INTERNATIONAL DESIGN CONFERENCE IN STOCKHOLM; FUTURE DESIGN DAYS, AND TO SPEAK TO THE PRESS FROM 20 COUNTRIES AROUND THE WORLD ON 'STYLE AND TRENDS IN MADRID' ORGANIZED BY SIEMENS. SHE HAS ALSO APPEARED TO DISCUSS CURRENT ISSUES IN THE WORLD OF FASHION AND ON TRENDS FOR CNN NEWS AND INTERVIEWS ON THE FOX NETWORK.

After a surprising personal call one morning from the Hollywood actress Rachel Weisz, asking Alexia to style her for the *Vanity Fair* Party at the Cannes Film festival, Alexia went on to dress her for public appearances and manage her personal wardrobe in the UK and US. Inspired by Rachel's comments about the 'fairy godmother-like' service she received, Alexia tailored a private styling and wardrobe management service called 'Diamond Dust' for those with more cash than dash. Alexia has styled numerous music videos over the years, but her best work came after being booked by Jake Nava to style videos for George Michael, Robbie Williams and Pink, as her work is geared towards 'big' characters and solo artists with a strong sense of style and most recently with Tinie Tempah and Travis Barker on a Lucozade campaign.

Alexia is currently based in Los Angeles, but works internationally, styling shows each season for various designers. In 2007 Alexia was appointed founding Fashion Director of *LUXURE* magazine, a prestigious luxury brand publication based in London and distributed worldwide. After four years of building the magazine, she left to return to freelancing, consulting and art directing for fashion brands and to pursue more challenging opportunities in the United States. She is a regular contributor to *Velour* magazine, and her 'Heroes and Villains' shoot by Nick Kelly was widely talked about on the Internet by fashion and image bloggers.

(LEFT) ALEXIA WORKS ON BOTH FASHION EDITORIAL SHOOTS AND (ABOVE) THESE HIGH FASHION IMAGES SHOW HER STYLING VERSATILITY

HOW DID YOU GET INTO THE FIELD?

After graduating she freelanced, working in graphics and web animation. Alexia began compiling a portfolio of test shoots with a photographer friend around 1997, at this time the scene in Hoxton exploded with lots of club kids and parties. She would dress up and attend and when asked what she did replied, "I'm a stylist" and began to build up contacts. Her friends in the Hoxton and Shoreditch areas were all in creative professions; hair stylists, makeup artists and they began working in teams on shoots. Alexia went on to meet Judy Blaine who commented on her striking platinum hair and offered Alexia her dream job. Through Judy and her mentor Pat McGrath she built up strong press contacts and began commissioning her own shoots. She once gate crashed a Chanel show to meet Patti Wilson – her platinum hair seemed to allow her access almost anywhere, she then sat in Patti's seat and when she arrived exclaimed, "I've been waiting for you – would you like to work with me?". She went on to work with Isabella Blow at *Tatler* and her career went from strength to strength.

DO YOU HAVE ANY TIPS FOR BUDDING STYLISTS?

She asks her interns if you weren't styling what would you be doing? If they answer within 30 seconds then they are in the wrong job. A stylist couldn't do anything else. Styling is all about drama and in order to earn a decent living you have to live and breathe it to succeed. To become a stylist do what comes naturally to you, don't copy someone else, resonate your personality and what comes from within. Copying is not style. If you do what comes naturally and incorporate your own personal style you should strive for people to say, "Wow I want to be that person." Dita von Teese dresses as her whole self and has a particular way about her that someone else just couldn't copy. Beth Ditto is another great example, she is fun and larger than life and her bold look shows this.

As an up and coming stylist – be aware of the industry, but be sure to live your life and then you can draw on your own experiences for your work. Lucinda Chambers of *Vogue* and Mario Testino both do this – he uses Africa a lot in his work and involving your interests adds layers to your work by including something you love. Alexia loves to include social and travel references.

ALEXIA STYLED THIS AMAZING FUTURISTIC SHOOT SHOT BY NICK KELLY SHOWING WHAT CAN BE ACHIEVED WITH STYLING TALENT AND IMAGINATION

WHO ARE YOUR MAIN CLIENTS?

Lucozade, Influx – constant work, *Tatler*, *Vogue*, Jason Priestly, Kristin Calavari, Robbie Williams, Pink, Pretty Polly, Vauxhall, L'Oreal

WHAT ARE YOUR FUTURE PLANS?

She is focusing on LA – working in costume, as a character stylist in the film industry and dressing celebrities. Alexia would love to do the complete wardrobe styling for a film and to have her own fashion line.

LIZZI
ZITA

www.myfashionreview.co.uk

BEACH IMAGES TAKEN WHILE LIZZI WAS ON A SHOOT WITH FRENCH *COSMOPOLITAN* AND (FAR RIGHT) A BEAUTIFUL CLOSE UP SHOT OF A KISS ON A FASHION SHOOT

Brief Biography

BORN IN LONDON TO ITALIAN/ HUNGARIAN PARENTS, LIZZI WAS BILINGUAL FROM A YOUNG AGE WITH A STRONG SENSE OF STYLE. HER PARENTS OWNED A SHOP WHERE THEY BOUGHT AND SOLD ITALIAN BAGS AND SHOES AND SHE HELPED OUT IN THE BUSINESS FROM CHILDHOOD. SHE WOULD REGULARLY VISIT MILAN AND FLORENCE BUYING ACCESSORIES FOR HER FAMILY BUSINESS. AS A CHILD SHE ADORED BEAUTIFUL THINGS AND BECAME INSPIRED BY FASHION MAGAZINES BEFORE STUDYING FASHION AND BEGINNING TO STYLE TEST SHOOTS. SHE SAYS 'I GOT MY POWERFUL WORK ETHIC FROM MY IMMIGRANT PARENTS WHO ARRIVED IN LONDON WITH NOTHING, BUILT A GOOD LIFE, AND PROVIDED AN EXCELLENT EDUCATION FOR MY SISTERS AND I THROUGH SHEER HARD WORK AND SELF BELIEF'.

AFTER GRADUATING FROM LONDON COLLEGE OF FASHION WITH A CERTIFICATE IN FASHION JOURNALISM, LIZZI CONTINUED BUYING FOR HER FAMILY'S ITALIAN CLOTHING BUSINESS SPENDING A LOT OF TIME SOURCING PRODUCTS IN ITALY. ON RETURNING TO LONDON, SHE STARTED WORKING ON TEST SHOOTS WITH YOUNG PHOTOGRAPHERS, SOME OF WHO WERE PUBLISHED BY *ID* MAGAZINE. SHE WENT ON TO WORK EDITORIALLY WITH THE *SUNDAY TIMES*, *THE TELEGRAPH*, AND EARLY EDITIONS OF *W*. SHE THEN BEGAN TO BUILD UP A BASE OF ADVERTISING CLIENTS INCLUDING LA PERLA AND MARKS AND SPENCER AS A LINGERIE AND HOSIERY STYLIST.

140

Since that time, Lizzi has worked successfully in the fashion industry as a props stylist for 20 years for top end magazines like *Vanity Fair*, *Glamour*, *Wig Magazine*, *The Telegraph*, *Cosmopolitan*, *Grazia* UK and Italian *Grazia*. She has been a personal stylist and image consultant for high-ranking members of Downing Street and a consultant with many professionals and wealthy individuals on creating powerful images and solving image related issues. In 2012 Lizzi founded www.myfashionreview.co.uk which is going from strength to strength. 'My Fashion Review is a place where people can give their opinions on their best fashion and beauty purchases'.

LOCATION SHOOT WITH FRENCH COSMOPOLITAN AND IN HUGE CONTRAST (OPPOSITE) A COLOUR POPPING STYLIZED SHOOT SHOWING THE POWER OF BRIGHT OUTFIT CHOICES

DO YOU HAVE ANY TIPS FOR BUDDING STYLISTS?

Learn the ropes by assisting a good stylist. Develop a reputation and work on building strong relationships with fashion PR companies by always attending launches and returning their calls and samples!

BRIEF OVERVIEW OF WHAT YOU DO?

Lizzi founded a fashion social media site, Style Frame, and regularly blogs about her opinions on both high street and catwalk fashion as well as working as a freelance stylist for several advertising clients and in props editorially. She has also dabbled in TV presenting both in the UK and Ireland.

WHAT ACHIEVEMENTS ARE YOU MOST PROUD OF?

Becoming a mother to my beautiful daughter Chiara and starting the website www.myfashionreview.co.uk

(BELOW) PROPS STYLING FOR *WIG* MAGAZINE, (CENTRE) A VIVID YELLOW JACKET MAKES THIS REFLECTION IMAGE WORK WELL ON THE FASHION SHOOT AND (FAR RIGHT) LIZZI AT NUMBER 10 DOWNING STREET AFTER STYLING A VIP CLIENT

MAIN CLIENTS AND PUBLICATIONS?

Lizzi has had a very varied client base from advertising clients which include Chloé, La Perla, Charnos, Marks and Spencer, Boots, The Body Shop, Dove, Oil of Olay, TK Maxx, Topshop, Wrigleys; to styling politicians and celebrities including Minnie Driver, Jerry Hall, Catherine Zeta Jones and supermodel Naomi Campbell.

Publications: Styling spreads for *Vanity Fair*, *The Sunday Times*, *The Telegraph*, Italian *Vogue*, *ID* Magazine, *The Face*, *Grazia*, *Wig*, *Frank*, *Harper's Bazaar*, French *Cosmopolitan*, *Tush* and American *Glamour*. Lizzi has also been a TV and radio presenter and fashion expert for fashion strands at the BBC, RTE Ireland, BBC Radio 2 and 4, Sky News, and The Vanessa Show.

WHAT ARE YOUR FUTURE PLANS?

Developing www.myfashionreview. co.uk and working with the internet and fashion to bring about environmental education and change. Also hopes to develop her own YouTube channel for her website.

STYLED BY (BELOW) CRYSTAL
DEROCHE AND (RIGHT)
ALEXIA SOMERVILLE

HOW TO BE YC

UR OWN
STYLIST

HOW TO
BE YOUR OWN
STYLIST

BOTH STYLED BY ROSA OSPINA

AS WE HAVE LEARNED, STYLING IS ALL ABOUT PERCEPTION. HOW THE CLIENT'S IMAGINATION IS BROUGHT TO LIFE IN A CREATION BY THE STYLIST TO BE PERCEIVED BY THE PUBLIC IN THE RIGHT WAY – BE IT FOR AN ADVERTISING CAMPAIGN, FASHION SHOW MUSIC VIDEO, RED CARPET OUTFIT OR SIMPLY DRESSING THE MOTHER OF THE BRIDE FOR A WEDDING.

On initially receiving a brief the stylist brainstorms outfit possibilities before approaching the client with ideas. This is the way we should approach our own personal style. Stylists should be able to look at themselves in the way they do a client and decide what looks good and what doesn't. Everyone has styles that suit them and ones that clearly don't, no two people are the same.

Experimenting to discover what you can and can't wear helps you create looks that you can carry off. Body shape and hair colour have a lot to do with how an outfit looks – the same dress on a short woman of size 16 will look completely different on a tall woman who wears a size 8. Our job as stylists is to achieve the optimum look by deciding what looks best. If hair colour or body shape changes then the colours and styles that can be carried off will also change; so weight loss or gain and colouring of hair can prompt huge wardrobe changes.

Underwear can make or break an outfit. A visible bra strap lump or VPL (visible panty line) can spoil a perfectly calculated outfit. I find nude underwear can take you anywhere and seamless knickers are as good an invention as the Spanx support pants. Strapless bras and support bras are also great investments in improving your body's shape inside your clothes. Tights can add a distinct look to an outfit, for example adding a cute printed pair to a plain dress. But they can easily spoil an outfit – coloured fishnets with your pencil skirt may just not cut it in the office.

Always check your outfit from in front and behind in a full length mirror. People see you at 360 degrees, so all angles need to be checked when creating your look.

When styling yourself it helps to have a core capsule wardrobe of basics that could stay in your closet for years and don't go out of date. Everyone needs a white shirt, black trousers, a black pencil skirt, a pair of well fitting jeans, an abundance of black dresses, a belted mac, winter coat, black court shoes, metallic sandals and a pair of knee high and ankle boots. These items can be added to – team a coloured cardigan with the little black dress or add a coloured tunic dress to the black trousers for night and a white shirt for day.

When your core investment pieces work well they should always be able to fit in with your new purchases. This season's must-have cropped top should work perfectly with your fitted jeans. The must-have IT bag of the season will sit along side your belted trench coat harmoniously. Hard working basics are worth spending a lot of money on, as they will stand the test of time. Trend pieces are more disposable so it makes sense to pay less for them.

HOW TO
BE YOUR OWN
STYLIST

ABOVE ALL WHEN BEING YOUR OWN STYLIST REMEMBER TO REFLECT YOUR OWN PERSONALITY. DON'T TRY TO COPY SOMEONE ELSE, BE TRUE TO YOURSELF AND IF YOU DO THIS WHATEVER THE OCCASION, WORK OR PLAY, YOU'RE GUARANTEED TO LOOK ELEGANT AND STYLISH.

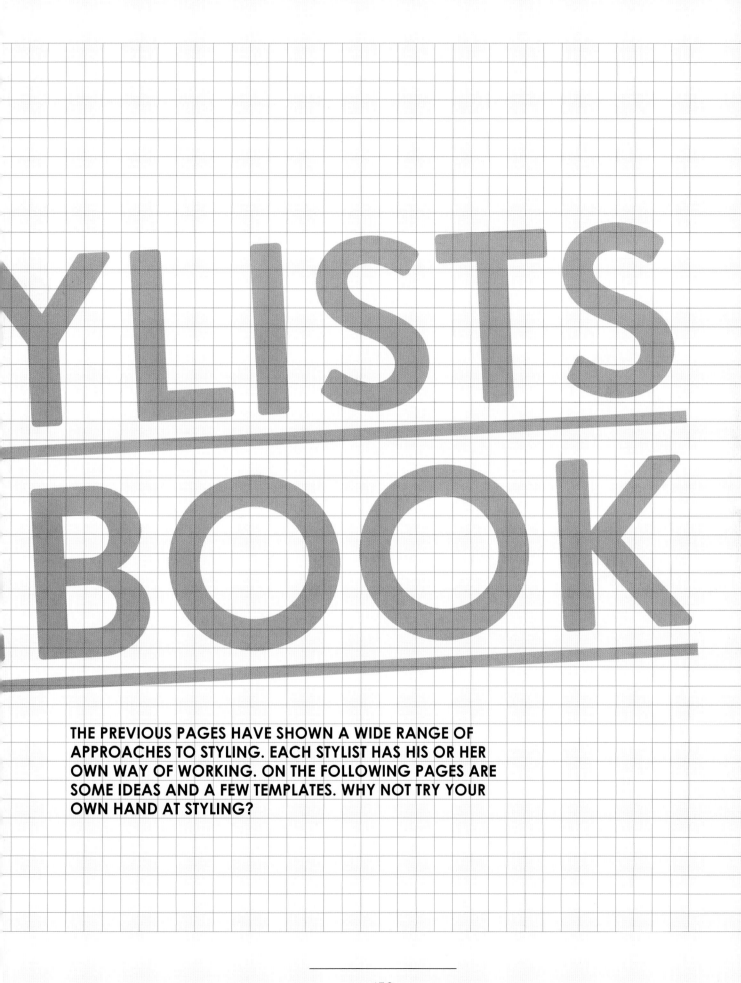

YLISTS
BOOK

THE PREVIOUS PAGES HAVE SHOWN A WIDE RANGE OF APPROACHES TO STYLING. EACH STYLIST HAS HIS OR HER OWN WAY OF WORKING. ON THE FOLLOWING PAGES ARE SOME IDEAS AND A FEW TEMPLATES. WHY NOT TRY YOUR OWN HAND AT STYLING?

IN TODAY'S MEDIA WORLD, WHOSE STYLE DO YOU MOST ADMIRE? WHY? WHAT IMAGE DO YOU THINK THEY ARE TRYING TO CONVEY?

☛ Create a mood board of ideas or images you think might reflect that person's style or, alternatively, how you might change their style.

☛ Cut out some ideas and images. Paste them here or put them on Pinterest.com

WHO WOULD YOU LIKE TO STYLE? WOULD YOU CHANGE THEIR STYLE? HOW WOULD YOU REFLECT BOTH THEIR PERSONALITY AND YOUR OWN SENSE OF STYLE? HERE IS A MALE FIGURE AND A FEMALE FIGURE TO HELP SPUR YOUR IMAGINATION.

THE CLIENT

A singer who wants to change her image.

THE BACKGROUND

For the last ten years, Angela has been
singing in musical theatre. While she has a
good reputation and a good stage presence,
she really wants to change her profile
and make it as a solo performer. A record
company has taken her on and changed her
name to 'Angel'. They have approached you
to complete the makeover and to create a
new persona for her new career.

MEDIA

They want you to create a look for her
new music video and her upcoming concert
tour. The record company can't decide
whether her look should be 'angelic' or just
the opposite.

Choose which way you want to style her,
do some research to help you create the
look and sketch some ideas that will work
for whichever mode you have chosen.

HERE IS THE OUTLINE FOR A DENIM JACKET. PART OF
STYLING IS SOMETIMES CREATING OR MODIFYING A
DESIGN ESPECIALLY FOR YOUR CLIENT. LET YOUR CREATIVE
JUICES FLOW AND CREATE A UNIQUE VERSION OF THIS
JACKET THAT MEETS YOUR CLIENT'S BRIEF.

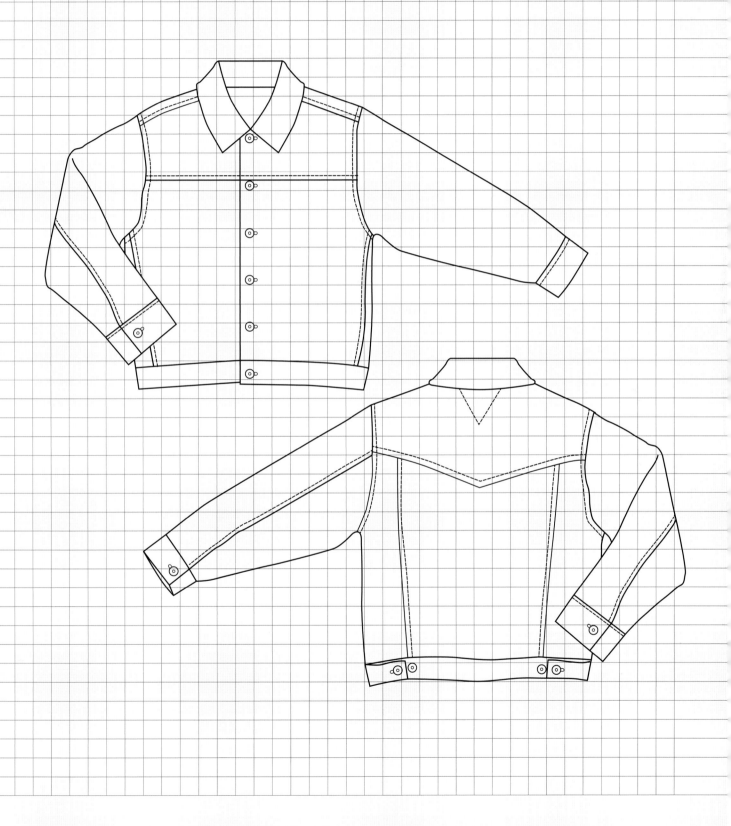

HERE IS A VERSATILE AND CLASSICAL LITTLE BLACK DRESS,
HOW WOULD YOU STYLE AND ACCESSORIZE THIS DRESS
FOR THE FOLLOWING SITUATIONS?

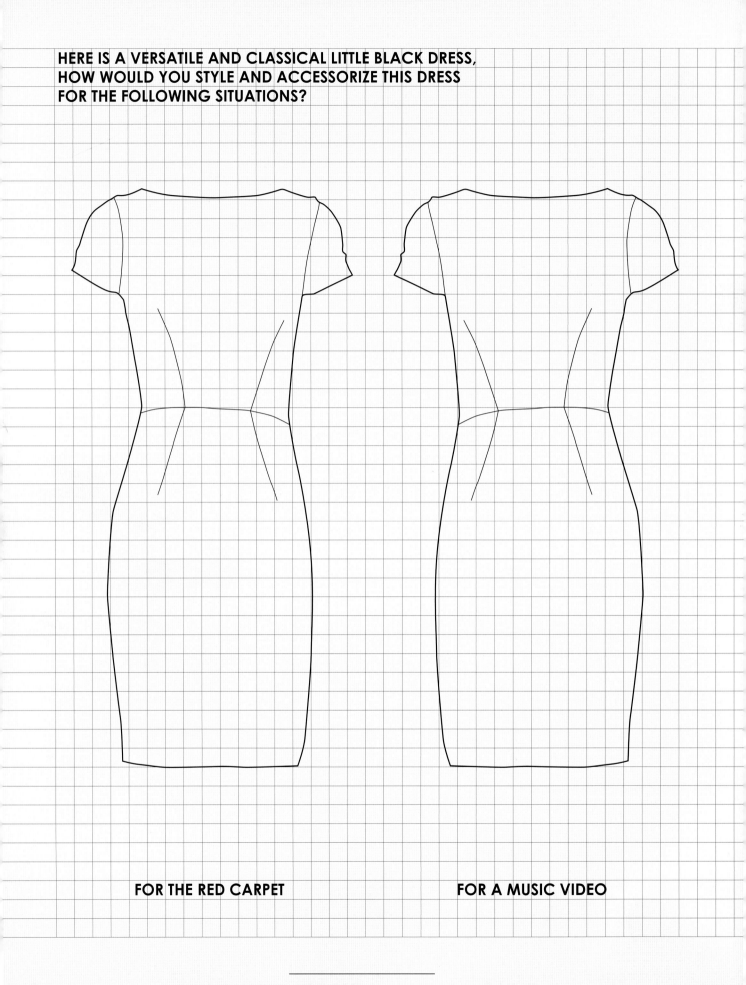

FOR THE RED CARPET

FOR A MUSIC VIDEO

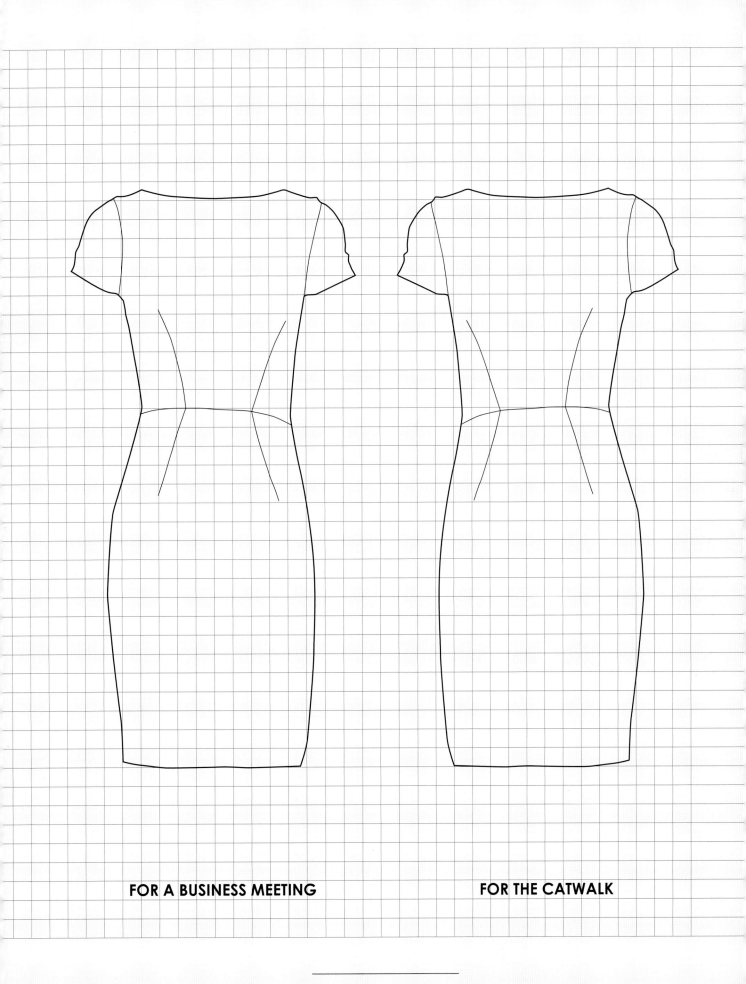

FOR A BUSINESS MEETING

FOR THE CATWALK

ACKNOWLEDGEMENTS

All I was ever going to do career-wise was go into fashion publishing and I knew this from a very young age. When I was a little girl my dad used to bring me home Disney Magazines, I then hit my teens and they quickly upgraded to Smash Hits hot off the press every week. My mam encouraged me to collect Sunday supplement magazines from The Telegraph when studying for my A-Levels and I dreamt of becoming the next Hilary Alexander. This led to a five year collection of Marie Claires once at university, which weighed as much as a small elephant!

I have had ten hugely enjoyable years in this crazy industry we call fashion and in that time I have had the pleasure of visiting wonderful places and working with some fantastic people. I was lucky enough to collaborate again with a lot of them again on this book and show the fashion industry is more than just playing dress-up: It can be really hard work. Thanks to them all for their time and allowing me to showcase the gems in their portfolios.

A huge thank you also to my family, especially my husband, Robin and daughter Meadow Isabella for their encouragement and Nicola Aimes and Sanjeeta Bains for their assistance with making sense of my notes and hours of Dictaphone recordings!

Not forgetting a massive thank you to Vivays Publishing especially the fantastic Lee Ripley for keeping me on track and Michael Lenz at Draught Associates for his patience and design expertise.

PICTURE CREDITS

EVERY EFFORT HAS BEEN MADE TO CREDIT THE APPROPRIATE SOURCE. PLEASE NOTIFY US IF THERE ARE ANY ERRORS OR OMISSIONS AND WE WILL PUT THEM RIGHT IN THE NEXT PRINTING. **A SPECIAL THANK YOU TO ALL OF THE STYLISTS AND PHOTOGRAPHERS WHO PROVIDED THE IMAGES FOR THIS BOOK.**

FRONT COVER: (main image) Main fashion-shoot for Star Magazine, Styled by Hershey Pascual, Photography by Caroline Leeming ; (top left) Futuristic shoot for Velour Magazine, Styled by Alexia Somerville, Photography by Nick Kelly; (bottom left) Cholo shoot for Attitude Magazine, Styling by Elauan Lee, Photography by Greg Vaughan; BACK COVER: (top right) Styling by Crystal Deroche, Photography by Marie Absolom; (bottom Left) Styling by Lizzi Zita, Photography by Heather Favell.

(Page 6) For None Magazine, Styling by Courtney Smith, Photography by Daniel Holfeld. (Pages 8-9) Styling by (top left) Alexia Somerville, Photography by Nick Kelly; (bottom) Styling by Rosa Ospina, Photography by Dragan Thomas; (opposite) Art Direction & Styling by Crystal Deroche, Makeup & Hair by Natalie Guest, Photography by Ade Okelarin "Asiko". (Pages 10-11) Styling by (left) Courtney Smith, Photography by German Collins; (right) Styling by Rosa Ospina, Photography by Christina Drosnan. (Pages 12-13) Styling by (left) Lizzi Zita, Photography by Carlos Lumiere; (right) Futuristic shoot for Velour Magazine, Styled by Alexia Somerville, Photography by Nick Kelly.(Page 15) Styling by Andrew Clancey, Photography by Richard Gerst. (Page 16) Merkezi shoot for OE magazine (Germany), Styling by Biki John, Model: Tatiana, Hair and Makeup: Servullo Mendez, Photography by Lars Borges. (Page 18 – 25) styling by Luanne McLean, Model: Carla Cressy, Photography by Tracy Morter. (Page 28) 'Bounty Hunters' for Attitude Magazine, Styling by Elauan Lee, Photography by Klas Strom; (below left) Art Direction Styling by Crystal Deroche, Makeup by Rocio Cordero, Hair by Magdalena Tucholska. Photography by Marie Absolom. (Page 31) Styling by Lizzi Zita, Photography by Heather Favell, Image for Star Magazine; (bottom right) Styling by Hershey Pascual, Photography by Caroline Leeming. (Page 33) Styling by Crystal Deroche, Makeup: Diana Asherson, Hair: Ciara McCarty, Photography by Imperia Staffieri. (Page 34) Styling by Carmen Haid, Photography © Atelier Mayer Magazine. (Page 35) Styling by Elauan Lee, Photography by Greg Vaughan. (Page 36) Styling by Courtney Smith, Photography by Daniel Holfeld. (Page 37) Styling by Biki John, Photography by Marcelo Benfield. (Page 38) Styling by Hershey Pascual, Photography by Caroline Leeming. (Page 39) Styling by Lizzi Zita, Photography by Daniel Ward. (Page 40) Styling by Courtney Smith, Photography by Daniel Holfeld. (Page 41) Styling by Farah Kabir, Photography by Stefan Lindeque. (Page 42) Styling by Rosa Ospina, Photography by Kestutis Anuzis. (Page 43) Styling by Alexia Somerville, Photography by Anthony Lycett. (Page 44) Styling by Chiara Solloa, Photography by Gary James. (Page 46) Profile pictures Courtesy of each stylist, personal photographs all rights reserved. (Page 48) Styling by Lupe Castro, Photography by Nico Dattani. (Page 49) Styling by Lupe Castro, Photography by Julia Mills Photography. (Page 50) Styling by Lupe Castro, Photography by Antoinette Castro. (Page 51) Styling by Lupe Castro, Photography by Arran Crinion. (Page 52) Styling by Andrew Clancey, Photograph courtesy of Andrew Clancey. (Page 53) Styling by Andrew Clancey. Photography by Tomo Kembery. (Page 54) Styling by Andrew Clancey, Photography by Frank Herholdt. (Page 56) Styling by Khaliah Clark, Photography courtesy of Khaliah Clark. (Page 57-59) Styling by Khaliah Clark, Photography by Andrew Clifton. (Page 60) Styling Joel Dash, (left) © Getty Images, Photography by Niki Nikolova. (Page 61) © Getty Images, (left) Photography by Jon Kopaloff, (right) Photography by Michael Buckner; (Page 62) © Getty Images, (top left) Photography by Jeff Vespa, (top right) Photography by Christopher Polk, (bottom left) Photography by Gary Gershoff, (bottom right) Photography Michael Loccisano, (Page 63) © Getty Images, (left) Photography by Nikki Houghton, (right) Photography by Dave M. Bennett. (Page 64) Art Direction & Styling by Crystal Deroche, Makeup & Hair by Natalie Guest, Photography by Ade Okelarin "Asiko". (Page 65) Art Direction & Styling by Crystal Deroche, Makeup by Rocio Cordero, Hair by Noriko Takayama, Photography by Marie Absolom. (Page 66) Styling by Crystal Deroche, Makeup by Rocio Cordero, Hair by Gigi, Photography by Hugh O'Malley. (Page 67) (top and bottom left) Art Direction & Styling by Crystal Deroche, Make up & Hair by Felicia Bonna, Photography by Reze Bonna, (right) Styling by Crystal Deroche, Photography by Marie Absolom. (Page 68) Art Direction & Styling by Crystal Deroche, Makeup by Sophie Fèvre, Hair by Mia Parker, Photography by Imperia Staffieri. (Page 69) (left) Styling by Crystal Deroche, Photography by Marie Absolom, (right) Art Direction & Styling by Crystal Deroche, Makeup by Rocio Cordero, Hair by Charl Marais, Photography by Charl Marais. (Pages 70-71) Styling by Carmen Haid, Photography by Chris Tubbs. (Page 72) Styling by Carmen Haid, Photography by Lucy Brown. (Page 73) Styling by Carmen Haid, Photography courtesy of Atelier Mayer magazine. (Pages 74-75) Styling by Carmen Haid, Photography by Phillippe Kliot. (Page 76) Styling by Biki John, Photography by David Fairweather. (Page 77) Zula shoot, Styling by Biki John, Model: Sosheba Griffiths. Makeup by Ken Nakano, Hair by Kunio Kohzaki, Photography by Marcelo Benfield. (Page 78) (left) 'The Morning After' shoot for Push It magazine (UK), Styling by Biki John, Model: Rebeka, Makeup by Ken Nakano, Hair by Akio Nishiyama, Photography by Piczo, (right) 'I'm not your Doll' shoot for Zoot magazine (Portugal), Styling by Biki John, Hair by Tomi Hirokono, Makeup by Ken Nakano, Photography by Marcelo Benfield. (Page 79) Styling by Biki John, Photography by David Merryweather. (Page 80) Styling by Biki John, Photography by Marcelo Benfield. (Page 81) 'The Flashpack' blog shoot, Styling by Biki John, Photography by Yusuke Miyazaki, Fashion Week pass, Photography courtesy of Biki John. (Page 82) (left) Image for Haya Mbc Magazine, Styling by Farah Kabir, Photography by Hussain Jian, (right) Styling by Farah Kabir, Image courtesy of Farah Kabir. (Page 83) (Main) Styling by Farah Kabir, Photography courtesy of Brownbook Magazine, (Insert) Styling by Farah Kabir, Photography courtesy of Friday Magazine. (Page 84) (top left) Image for Friday magazine, Styling by Farah Kabir, Photography by Grace Paras, (bottom left) Image for Alpha magazine,Styling by Farah Kabir, Photography by Silvia Barron, (bottom middle) Image for Friday magazine, Styling by Farah Kabir, Photography by Grace Paras, (bottom right) for Friday Magazine, Styling by Farah Kabir, Photography by Garth Stead. (Page 85) (main) Image for Friday Magazine, Styling by Farah Kabir, Photography by Grace Paras, (top left) Styled by Farah Kabir, Courtesy of Farah Kabir. (Page 86) (main) image for Friday Magazine, Styling by Farah Kabir, Photography by Grace Paras and Garth Stead, (top right) Styling by Farah Kabir, Photography courtesy of Friday Magazine, (bottom right) Styling by Farah Kabir, Photography courtesy of Cartier. (Page 87) (bottom left) Styling by Farah Kabir, Photography courtesy of Brownbook Magazine, (top left) Image for Friday Magazine, (centre) Image for Friday Magazine, Styling by Farah Kabir, Photography by Stefan Lindeque, (right) Image for Friday Magazine, Styling by Farah Kabir, Photography by Grace Paras. (Page 88) courtesy JILF for Attitude Magazine, Styling by Elauan Lee, Photography by Elvis Di Fazio. (Page 89) Daniel Radcliffe Cover feature for Attitude Magazine, Styling by Elauan Lee, Photography by Greg Vaughan.(Pages 90-91) Main image for Attitude Magazine, Styling by Elauan Lee, Photography by Cameron McNee, (Insert) Styling by Elauan Lee, Photography by Misha Taylor. (Page 92) Cholo for Attitude Magazine, Styling by Elauan Lee, Photography by Greg Vaughan. (Page 93) 'Bounty Hunters' as seen in Attitude Magazine, Styling by Elauan Lee, Photography by Klaus Strom. (Page 94-97) Styling by Zoe Lem. Photography by Anne Brassier. (Page 98) (left) Adidas for River Island, Styling by Arieta Mujay, Hair by Lisa Laudet, Makeup by Tania Courtney, Photography by Felix Cooper, (right) Pacha for River Island, Styling by Arieta Mujay, Photography courtesy of Pacha for River Island. (Page 99) Adidas for River Island, Styling by Arieta Mujay, Hair by Lisa Laudet, Makeup by Tania Courtney, Photography by Felix Cooper. (Page 100) (top left) Paloma Faith,Styling by Arieta Mujay, Photography by Diana Gomez,(bottom left) Pacha for River Island, Styling by Arieta Mujay, Photography courtesy of Pacha for River Island. (Page 101) Adidas for River Island, Styling by Arieta Mujay, Hair by Lisa Laudet, Makeup by Tania Courtney, Photography by Felix Cooper. (Page 102) 'Factory Girl', Styling by Rosa Ospina, Photography by Rohan Reiley. (Page 103) courtesy Alice Halliday Designs, Styling by Rosa Ospina, Photography by Kestutis Anuzis . (Page 104) Styling by Rosa Ospina, Photography by Rohan Reiley. (Page 105) All three images courtesy of Sharon Rose Designs, Styling by Rosa Ospina, Photography by Ger Murphy. (Page 106) Both Images, Styling by Rosa Ospina, Photography by Lisa O Dwyer. (Page 107) Both Images courtesy Alice Halliday, Styling by Rosa Ospina, Photography by Micki Darlok. (Pages 108-109) Images for Star Magazine, Styling by Hershey Pascual,Photography by Gianni Diliberto. (Page 110) (left) Westlife for Star Magazine, Styling by Hershey Pascual, Photography by Neil Cooper, (right) Ricky Gervais for Star Magazine, Styling by Hershey Pascual, Photography courtesy of Northern and Shell, shot by Paul Wesolek. (Page 111) All three images for Star Magazine, Styling by Hershey Pascual, Photography by Amar Daved. (Page 113) Styling by Nikki Pennie, Photography courtesy of People magazine, The Hollywood Reporter and Harper's Bazaar. (Page 114 and 115) Styling by Nikki Pennie, Photography courtesy of People magazine. (Page 116-119) Kelly Rowland images, (left) Photography Alex Gaudino for Kelly Rowland 'What a Feeling' music video, Styling by Kalvin Ryder, Director and choreography: Frank Gatson, Producers Melissa Moore, Jack Hogan and Josh Goldstein. (Page 117) courtesy Aylar images, 'Hard2Beat' ft Aylar ' Some People' music video, Styling by Kalvin Ryder, Photography courtesy of Hard2beat records. (Page 118) Basshunter, Styling by Kalvin Ryder, Director Alex Herron, Photography courtesy of Ultra Records.(Page 121) (top left) Image for Thread Magazine, Styling by Angela Scanlon, Photography by Liam Murphy, (bottom right) Styling by Angela Scanlon, Photography by Rebecca Nean. (Page 122) Styling by Angela Scanlon, Photography by Johnny McMillan. (Page 123) Both images, Styling by Angela Scanlon, Photography by Johnny Savage. (Pages 124-125) Styling by Courtney Smith, Photography by Daniel Holfeld. (Page 126) Styling by Courtney Smith, Photography by German Collins. (Page 127) Styling by Courtney Smith, Photography by Daniel Holfeld. (Pages 128-129) (left) Styled by Chiara Solloa, Picture courtesy of Chiara Solloa, (centre) Styled by Chiara Solloa, Photography by Theo Samuels, (right) Styled by Chiara Solloa, © Chiara Solloa. (Pages 130-131) Styled by Chiara Solloa, Photography by Theo Samuels. (Pages 132-133) (main) Styled by Chiara Solloa, Photography by Theo Samuels, (right) Styled by Chiara Solloa, Music video directed by Jesse Terrero (Page 134) Styling by Alexia Somerville, Photography by Erica Bergsmeds. (Page 136-137) Images for Tatler, Styling by Alexia Somerville, Photography by Robert Astley-Sparke. (Pages 137-139) Images for Velour Magazine, Styling by Alexia Somerville, Photography by Nick Kelly. (Page 140) Both Images, Styling by Lizzi Zita, Photography by Chris Craymer. (Page 141) Styling by Lizzi Zita, Photography by Seb Winter. (Page 142) (left) Styling by Lizzi Zita, Photography by Daniel Ward, (centre) Styling by Lizzi Zita, Photography by Heather Favell, (right) Styling by Lizzi Zita, Photography by Daniel Ward. (Page 143) Styling by Lizzi Zita, Photography by Seb Winter. (Pages 144-145) (bottom left) Image for Wig Magazine, Props styling by Lizzi Zita, Photography by Felix Lammers, (centre) Styling by Lizzi Zita, Photography by Seb Winter, (top right) Styling by Lizzi Zita, Photography courtesy of Lizzi Zita. (Page 146) Art Direction & Styling by Crystal Deroche, Photography by Reze Bonna, Makeup & Hair by Felicia Bonna. (Page 147) Cover shot for first edition of Luxure Magazine, Styling by Alexia Somerville, Photography courtesy of Luxure Magazine. (Page 148) Styling by Rosa Ospina, Photography by Rohan Reiley. (Page 149) Styling by Rosa Ospina, Photography by Michael Stephens. (Page 150) Styling by Courtney Smith, Photography by Daniel Holfeld.